FIERCE STYLE

HOW TO BE YOUR MOST FABULOUS SELF

CHRISTIAN SIRIANO

WITH RENNIE DYBALL

FOREWORD BY TIM GUNN

ORIGINAL PHOTOGRAPHY BY BRAD WALSH

GC

GRAND CENTRAL PUBLISHING

New York Boston

Photo credits are located on page 243.

Grand Central Publishing
Hachette Book Group
237 Park Avenue
New York, NY 10017

Visit our Web site at www.HachetteBookGroup.com.

Printed in the United States of America

First Edition: October 2009
10 9 8 7 6 5 4 3 2 1

Grand Central Publishing is a division of Hachette Book Group, Inc.
The Grand Central Publishing name and logo is a trademark of
Hachette Book Group, Inc.

Library of Congress Cataloging-in-Publication Data
Siriano, Christian.
Fierce style: how to be your most fabulous self / Christian Siriano with Rennie Dyball.—1st ed.
p. cm.
ISBN 978-0-446-54601-0
1. Clothing and dress. 2. Women's clothing. 3. Shopping. 4. Fashion. I. Dyball, Rennie. II. Title.
TT507.S657 2009
646.4'04—dc22 2009006080

Design by Joel Avirom and Jason Snyder

For my mother, family, friends,
and all you aspiring artists!

(FABULOUS!)

CONTENTS

FOREWORD

My first impression of Christian Siriano wasn't a great one. To be fair, we hadn't met face to face yet: It was the spring of 2007, and I was looking at his audition profile for *Project Runway*—a stack of paper about twenty pages thick. I fast-forwarded to the education section, as I always do. We don't ask for would-be contestants' ages on the show, so the education section reveals something about their age and experience. And Christian Siriano had just graduated from design school.

"*Why* are we seeing this guy?" I asked my producers and fellow judges. "He's a kid! He can't possibly compete." We had already cast a number of very experienced designers and we'd been saying no, generally, to anyone who had recently graduated from design school. The producers told me that Christian had already passed the prescreening process, so we may as well see him. Said a producer, "Maybe the whole thing will take about ten seconds and he'll be out of here."

In fact, it did take about ten seconds. It took me that long to recognize just how talented Christian was. He had not even opened his mouth. He was still holding the garments that he brought in when I turned to the judges and said, "Look at this work!" And upon speaking to him, I declared that this was an old soul. This was not a twenty-one-year-old kid. In thirty years of teaching, working with young people, and launching careers, I had never met a fashion prodigy until I met Christian.

From the onset of his time on *Runway*, it was nothing but "wow" moments. It was the ambitiousness of his ideas and his deft ability to execute them. I would see his sketches and think, "How is *this* going to happen?" And shortly I learned, well, it *is* going to happen. And it's going to happen consistently. There's exuberance in his designs—nothing is ever a basic silhouette. It's *all* about the details. And he takes enormous risks. What

I love about risk taking is that it is how great work comes about—greatness doesn't come from playing it safe.

That's why, to me, Christian epitomizes a fashion designer as opposed to a clothing designer. There are lots of people who can design beautiful clothes, but a fashion designer is an altogether different breed. They are almost barometric gauges of this culture, so their work comes out of a context that's societal and historical and political. That's why fashion always changes in a way that clothes don't need to. We *need* clothes—we don't *need* fashion. But I do think we need Christian Siriano.

Beyond what he brings to the runways, Christian has lessons to teach others, even at such a young age. First off, if you're going to portray yourself as fierce, you better really *be* fierce and have the goods to back it up! I will say, very candidly, that Christian's disposition in the *Project Runway* workroom could become very grating. There were times that I just wanted to haul off and smack him! But he *always* delivered the goods. Sure, he was full of pomp and circumstance and bravado, but he had the work to back it up. (And in truth, he really is a wonderful individual—lovable, smart, funny, witty, and, really, a sweetheart.)

And then there's his fearless approach to life. Feeling and acting fierce, as Christian would say, allows you to walk through doors that you wouldn't otherwise walk through and almost always begets new experiences. You never know where life is going to take you, and you've got to be fierce and fearless about that. Open that door that's closed at the moment and see what's behind it. You can always take another route.

Finally, if anyone is wondering exactly what "fierce" means, I'll offer my own definition. (Christian will define it for you later, as well.) To me, "fierce" is something that's undeniably and in-your-face great. There's nothing remotely subtle about things that are fierce. Like Christian himself! It's a word with potent meaning, and one that I can't help but use. When I would greet Christian at his worktable on the show, I would always begin by asking of his design, "Okay, how fierce is it?"

I hope you enjoy Christian's book. Maybe looking, feeling, and acting fierce isn't right for everybody, but I do believe there are a lot of people who should strive to attain fierceness. Because it's self-perpetuating—if you're fierce in life, you're going to stay that way! Who wouldn't want that? And there's no one better to learn from than the person who defines and personifies it.

Yours in fabulosity,

Tim Gunn

INTRODUCTION

What up, divas!? Ever since I won *Project Runway*, people have been asking me about one thing: being fierce. Sure, they talk about my clothes, too. (Obviously. Hello!) But the more people I meet, the more I realize that they're also interested in how I became the person I am today. So what exactly does it mean to be fierce? Let me paint you a little picture . . .

It's September 11, 2008, and I'm presenting my first full collection at Fashion Week. Right before the show begins, I am backstage with all my models, adjusting hats and shoes and checking straps and hemlines. (I'm looking flawless, too, of course, in a classic Christian outfit: black tee, gray vest, black skinny jeans.) My collection—a sea of grays, blues, and yellows—dances around me. It's months of hard work come to life, and I stop, for just a moment, to take it all in. This is exactly what I've always wanted and I'm actually living it. I worked hard, took risks and took chances, and I'm about to show my first full collection at Fashion Week! But there's no time to reflect now. I have to get back to fixing all the last-minute snags that keep cropping up: a wrong shoe here, a change of hairstyle there. I can barely hear the music pumping outside or the chatter of attendees awaiting my show. I can't hear anything, really; it's all just a soundless, surreal blur. Then Heidi breezes in to wish me good luck. (Heidi Klum! Who knew?) We exchange air kisses (both cheeks) and she heads back out toward her seat, blending into the maze of models.

And just like that, it's showtime. I feel like I'm holding my breath for all twenty-eight looks. I can hear applause, even cheering, but I'm still a nervous wreck. But before I know it, the show is over. And it went off flawlessly. The crowd and the press alike loved my work. Well-wishers and cameras and reporters flood the backstage area. I accept dozens more air kisses, compliments, and hugs. I really did it.

So, why did I just share that little story with you? Because *that*, my divas, is what it means to have fierce style—inside and out. It's feeling fabulous about yourself, being strong, independent, and confident in what you do (all while looking totally ferosh, of course!). It's about making things happen and tackling one challenge after the next. My hope is that you will find something in the following pages, whether it's about clothes or something else, that inspires you to be fierce yourself. Big or small, silly or serious, I hope you take away some inspiration.

And if you're wondering what exactly "ferosh" means, don't worry. Confused about the difference between "tickity tack" and "hot tranny mess"? You're probably not alone! Just consult page 227 for the official Christian Siriano Glossary. As they joked about me on *Saturday Night Live,* I sometimes have my own private language. (Disclaimer: "Fierce" should be used somewhat sparingly or it can quickly feel played out—even *I* know that. Once, right after *Runway*, a waiter at a French restaurant asked me, in his thick accent, "Was the food fierce?" I almost died.) So keep an eye out for a cute little star (*) next to all my words and catchphrases the first time they show up in each chapter and check out what they mean in the glossary.

Finally, as you may know, I look up to some of the most flawless people in Hollywood. And, get this, they actually like *me*, too! So they'll share with you their own fearless tips about style, confidence, and how to act like a superstar throughout the book. Fabulous, right? What up.

XOXO
Christian

PART ONE

Lady, You Look Fabulous!!!!

Looking fierce* is the obvious place to start. After all, people notice how you look before they notice much else. And finding your own look is more than just aesthetics—your clothes and your personal style make a statement to the world. Don't you want to control whether the world sees you as ferosh* or a hot tranny mess?* I thought so!

1 FINDING YOUR PERSONAL STYLE

Finding your personal style is a process, people. Fabulous* fashionistas aren't born—they're made. You didn't think I always knew to rock my signature look of skinny jeans and my fashion-hawk hairstyle, did you? Hell, no! It may be hard to believe, but I was once as tickity tack* as they come. Trust.* So to start the hunt for your own fabulous look, try out the following.

Reminisce, Darling!

If you're trying to find your own look and personal style, recall what you loved as a child. What got your imagination going? What were your very favorite things? Your childhood obsessions are *not* exempt from influencing your adult fashion sensibilities, so remember what you loved back then. It can be a great way to get your look started.

Growing Up Fabulous

If you were really artistic and loved to paint, the boho chic look may be perfect for you. Try some long skirts or dresses (Old Navy is a good place to start shopping, as are department stores like Neiman Marcus or Bloomingdale's), or add artsy touches to your clothing like a blouse with intricate details or textured fabrics, beading, patchwork, or embroidery.

If you rode horses when you were little, you might gravitate toward clothes with an equestrian flair now, like fitted blazers and knee-high boots (either flat or with a small, squared-off heel) to wear over leggings or jeans. Check out stores like Gap, J.Crew, or Banana Republic for blazers; Steve Madden or department stores for boots.

FEARLESS TIP: *Thinking back on your interests as a kid can be a great starting place for developing your look today.*

If sports were your thing, today you might like athletic touches in your look. There are tons of cute sneakers out there—Puma makes great, creative recreation styles. A pair of sneakers in fun colors, like fuchsia and black, or white and a touch of gold, can really jazz up an otherwise casual outfit.

If you were a theater-loving kid with a flair for the dramatic, you might be drawn to unexpected, high-impact looks like over-sized collars or striking jewelry. Urban Outfitters has fun, inexpensive accessories, like big earrings and long beaded necklaces. A top from Urban with a pattern print and bold color is another good bet, or a pair of jeans in an unusual color, like purple or red, could be fun as well (though I still love classic black skinny jeans to offset a dramatic top).

Maybe you've always been a real girlie-girl—the type of kid who would never go anywhere unless she was in a party dress. Today, your options for dressing in really feminine looks are endless! Romantic styles, like florals, lace, and ruffles are always girly and flirty. You can find ruffled dresses pretty much anywhere, but some good brands to start with include bebe, Rebecca Taylor, and Milly. And you can always go über-feminine in your accessories. If you want to step it up a notch on the sophistication scale, there is nothing more ladylike than a strand of pearls or two.

And finally, for you former tomboys out there, you might embrace a menswear-inspired look today. A wide-leg trouser pant (available in tons of places—check out H&M or department stores like Nordstrom, and Christian Siriano Spring 2009, of course) paired with a white button-down shirt can be a fun way to dress in a typically masculine look. Just be sure to add a feminine touch. You're not a rough-and-tumble kid anymore, lady!* Add a chic heel or a pair of beaded earrings to your outfit.

I bet you can see hints of your childhood in the clothes and accessories you're attracted to today. I know that I can!

Following the Yellow Brick Road

The Wizard of Oz was one of my earliest inspirations and childhood loves. I was about four years old when I first saw it, and, immediately, I was swept up into the fantasy world of Oz. I was *all* about those costumes: Scarecrow and Tin Man and the Munchkins, oh my! I was hooked. There was so much to see and soak in: Glinda's tiered, ruffled ball gown! Dorothy's blue gingham and ruby-red heels! The Winged Monkeys' textured jackets! I was obsessed. Watched it dozens, no, *bazillions* of times.

I also loved playing dress-up as a kid, especially when it meant turning into the characters from Oz. But that became a bit of a problem when I wanted to dress up *all* the time! Every day after school, I transformed myself into the Scarecrow and the Tin Man and Dorothy and Glinda. My mom says she remembers me always having a stick in my hand but it was actually a yellow plastic ax. (Because the Tin Man carried one, hello!?) Or I'd carry a

basket for Toto, just like Dorothy. I was always with a prop—like John Galliano and his cane!

The biggest dress-up occasion of them all was, of course, Halloween. October thirty-first was like a giant fashion show for me: I would have fifteen different costumes for a single year (including every character from Oz, of course), and I'd run home and change after I'd worn each costume and head back out. (That also meant hitting each house in the neighborhood multiple times in my multiple costumes, so I had one big candy haul!) I was working the runway—well, the sidewalks—at age five.

But soon, just playing dress-up wasn't enough. I wanted to *perform.* So I put on plays for my family and neighbors in my house—we had these orangey stones in our hallway, so I made them into the Yellow Brick Road. I invited all the children in the neighborhood over and we'd re-create *The Wizard of Oz* for the grown-ups. I was hooked on the costumes and the drama of it all. And I can tell today that my love for performance and for that movie has seeped into my style and design aesthetic, since I always try to incorporate drama into my work: At the end of my Spring 2009 show, for example, I had crazy, oversized hats and a bright orange flounce dress, and I closed the show with a floor-length gown of blue and gray ruffles. Fabulous!

My other early obsession was Aerosmith. Steven Tyler's rock-star style—his punky, feminine look of scarves, supertight jeans, vests, and weird pointy-toed boots—brought out my inner rock star. I also became infatuated with a pair of leather chaps he once wore—they even inspired my design for the WWE divas challenge on *Project Runway*! Today, my everyday style is a bit like Steven Tyler's: skinny jeans, vests, scarves, pointy-toed boots.

Get Inspired!

So once you're done reminiscing, try these exercises.

Read Up

Say you don't know your Missoni from your Manolo Blahnik or your L.A.M.B. from your Louis Vuitton. Fashion magazines are a great place to start learning. Go buy a few, like *Elle*, *Vogue*, or *Nylon*—or, if you're younger, *Seventeen* or *Teen Vogue*. (And for you fashionistas, check out *I.D.*, *Paper*, *Surface*, and *Zink*!) Look at the trends they're showing and pick one that you want to try—something that's popular and that catches your eye. If it's spring, you might choose a scarf around the neck that's soft and feminine, or a long dress. Then start shopping for that piece. And then go back to the magazines and pick another trend to try out. Go to tons of different stores with prices in different ranges and just have fun with it. Trends are hardly the most important thing in fashion (especially the ones that come and go in the blink of an eye), but they're a good place to start if you're new to all of this. Before you

FEARLESS TIP:
It's important to look to the present. Pop culture and your current interests can impact your fashion sense today.

know it, you'll be picking up on brands and designers, learning what looks good on you, and, hopefully, loving fashion—and soon, creating your own trends!

Chitty Chat

Another easy way to get inspired is by talking to people about their clothes. If you love the way someone at your office dresses, start chatting with him or her about where they bought their top or their jeans. You don't necessarily have to buy (window-shopping, hello!) but the more often you look at—and try on—clothes, the easier it will be for you to create your own look.

Look to Pop Culture

Movies, books, and TV are great places from which to draw inspiration. Are you crazy about the way the *Gossip Girl* divas dress? Then try copying one of their looks in a general way. (You don't have to buy every designer piece, of course!) If you love Blair's prim and preppy look, go buy a polo shirt in a fun, bright color or a little striped sweater from Lacoste or Ralph Lauren. Or hit up an Urban Outfitters or Anthropologie for a cute headband (Blair's signature!). You can do the same with characters from books and movies, too. If you love the way someone dresses, try to emulate it.

My friends do that all the time. And I particularly love when they take ideas from music videos. Rihanna wears suspenders and a funky hat in one of her videos, so a friend of mine had fun re-creating that look for a night out. And the best part is he is a boy!! So take those risks and have fun with it.

Learn from Your Mistakes

Remember: No one is born with a flawless* fashion sense, and most of us cringe when we look back on our own personal fashion evolution. Everyone has those old photos that would land them on any worst-dressed list. You don't need a magazine to tell you what not to wear—just look at old pictures of yourself for a customized list of what does *not* work for you! Do you think you looked ridiculous in high school in your bell-bottom jeans? Now you know to stick with a straight-leg or skinny style. Used to (regrettably) wear red every day? Now you know that natural tones work better for you. But whatever your missteps, don't worry. Everyone's made mistakes. I've probably made more than most.

FEARLESS TIP:* *While fashion missteps are embarrassing in hindsight, you can use them as your own personal list of fashion don'ts.

Childhood Tassels

Some of my personal fashion don'ts came from growing up in Annapolis, Maryland, where you can't escape the nautical style—it's a boat town, plain and simple. As I got older I'd make fun of everyone in their boat shoes with the tassels. But I started out in those! It was slip-on boat shoes *every* day for me. Then there was the striped period: striped shorts, striped boat shoes, and striped T-shirts. So bad! But I couldn't be stopped. If it had stripes on it, I had to have it—in every color.

The Confused Years

By middle school, I'd done a total one-eighty. Boat shoes be gone! Instead, I traded them for FUBU jerseys, huge baggy jeans, and New Balance sneakers. Remember the big-logo Tommy Hilfiger and Nautica T-shirts that were popular back then? I had dozens. Those were bad days. I was a little white fairy kid walking around in giant FUBU jerseys. Tough times!

Label Obsessions

By high school, I was all about the Armani Exchange T-shirts with the big logos. As far as I was concerned, they were totally fabulous. I had more than I could count. So gross. Wearing labels like that is pretty overdone. There's just no need to advertise what brand you're wearing—that shouldn't matter. What does matter is how things look on you, whether they're from Goodwill or Gucci. (Labels do matter, but it's a matter of quality, not showing off a brand.) And when I wasn't wearing A/X, it was Abercrombie and Fitch, American Eagle, Guess, Tommy Hilfiger, and Nautica everywhere! I couldn't enter a room without people reading me. Literally. That is probably my worst fashion memory.

Oh, and another awful part of my high school look? I wore *wire*-rimmed glasses! Whoa, stay away. Wire frames are not cute for anyone. They're gross. If you have them, throw them away. Seriously, I'll wait.

The London Fog

When I moved to London for college, I wore this *floor-length* white trench coat all the time (seriously—*floor*-length!), pointy-toed boots, and huge spiky hair. All the time. I looked like a horrible tranny!* I thought they were fabulous and fashionable. But to everyone else, I must have looked so scary. I thought I *was* fashion. But really, I was just overdoing it. A high-impact piece like a floor-length trench coat really should be worn sparingly. And though pointy-toed boots can work from time to time, it's usually a good idea to mix it up when it comes to footwear.

While we're on the topic of fashion faux pas . . .

10 Things ***Not*** to Wear ***If*** You Want to Be Fabulous

1. ***Wire-frame glasses.*** Ugh, they are not cute, ever. They do nothing for your face! Instead: Buy a thick, fabulous plastic frame to frame your face. Tortoise-shell only.

2. ***UGG boots.*** They make your legs look like stippity stumpies. Instead: Wear heels, lady! I love a mile-high heel, but any height will do, really. Pumps are great. Mary Janes, stilettos, platforms, wedges—it's all good. There's just no need for UGGs; not only are they flat, but they're bulky and broad. Do your legs a favor and wear some warm leather boots.

3. ***Flip-flops.*** Oh my God, they're so boring! I'm over it. Instead: If you want to be comfortable, get a chic sandal (strappy, shiny ones in gold or silver are fun for summer; if you want to go more basic, black and strappy always works—just don't go overboard with the gladiator look) or a great-looking flat (look for a fun detail on the toe, like a fringe or a buckle—I *love* Tory Burch flats).

4 ***Shapeless jeans.*** You may as well be wearing a denim sack. Instead: a distinct style in denim that works for your body—whether it be skinny, wide-leg, or high-waisted jeans. It doesn't matter where you get the jeans, as long as they've got a shape. Dark denim is almost always best.

5 ***Sweatpants.*** Again, not flattering. Find a way to stay comfy without sacrificing the way you look. Instead: Puma or Stella McCartney track pants.

6 ***Hoodies.*** They make you look frumpy and sloppy (unless they're fitted and detailed). Instead: A hooded sweater is much more chic. It can zip up, button, or tie in the front.

Fearless (Celebrity!) Tip

"Fight the frump! I think when people aren't feeling great, they tend to hide in frumpy clothing. I used to do it, too. I would wear the biggest, oldest sweatshirt with huge sweatpants and big, fuzzy warm boots when I was having a bad day. But no matter how much you try to hide, people can still see you. When you feel frumpy on the inside, you have to fight it on the outside. Throw out the sweats (they are *never* appropriate) and put on something cute!"

—*UGLY BETTY*'S BECKI NEWTON

7 ***Big logos.*** Cheesy! Instead: Go label free (unless it's something classic and super chic, like Louis Vuitton). You should know a designer by their clothes' shape and the style, not the logo. That is just tick-tack-toe.*

8 ***Baseball hats.*** They don't look good on anyone! (Except David Beckham, and only David Beckham.) Instead: a more stylish hat, like a fedora. Or just pull your hair back into a chic, slicked-back bun.

9 ***Fabric band watches.*** Too cheap looking. Instead: something sleek, pretty, and simple, like leather.

10 ***Polyester fabrics.*** Ugh, so tickity tack!* Instead: any other fabrics, really (e.g., cotton jersey, silk or wool crepe). Polyester doesn't lie right and it's too shiny. You'll look far better in something else.

Fearless (Celebrity!) Tip

"Don't wear *anything* that shows your stomach."

—NIKI TAYLOR

(Sorry, trannies,* but there's so much bad stuff out there that I'm gonna have to go a bit longer with this listy-list.)

11 ***Fleece jackets.*** They are just so shapeless and sloppy looking. Instead: Buy a real jacket! Get something more tailored—like a peacoat or a trench—and lined for the cold.

12 ***Fake leather.*** Instead: Always buy the real stuff. Pleather is shiny and doesn't breathe. That is always a hot tranny mess.*

2 THE DOS AND DON'TS

These are the golden rules of looking fierce. Follow them and you'll have an easier time shopping and putting together a fabulous outfit every morning!

Do: Take Chances!

When you're figuring out where you fit on the fashion spectrum, try to experiment. And do play around with fashion at any age. Any mom or dad, grandma or grandpa, out there who wants to mix it up is *fabulous*.*

My own experimentation with fashion began in my sophomore year of high school, when I started working at Bubbles salon in Annapolis, Maryland. So much of who I am today comes from my time at Bubbles. I went from dressing like most of the people in my preppy town (can you imagine?!) to expanding my fashion horizons in a big way. I spent my days surrounded by crazy, fun people in the salon who would wear the wackiest things, and I wanted to look just like them. At one point, I was wearing mesh shirts from Hot Topic and sequined pants with zippers all over them. (Oh my God, I was so gay!)

Looking back, when I worked at Bubbles I actually had a terrible sense of fashion. I thought I was totally cool, working at a really trendy salon and wearing the craziest things I could get my hands on. Not so cute! But when you take chances, you learn what works and what looks good on you, and you get to try on different personas.

FEARLESS TIP: *Whether you consider yourself preppy or punky, conservative or crazy, don't put yourself in one fashion box.*

Bubbles was nothing like the outside world. The people were so inspiring to me. They were fashionable and fabulous, and one of the main reasons I became interested in clothes. I'd always ask them what they were wearing and where they bought their clothes because they looked so different from most people in my prepster town. I was obsessed with everything I saw, and even though I didn't always get it right, I tried things on, in every sense of the word, and continued building my look.

Don't: Wear Fakes

Simply put, fakes are cheesy. They're just not worth it. If you have the money to buy a fabulous designer item, that's great. If not, there are infinite ways to look fabulous without breaking the bank. So there's really no need to wear a phony designer piece. (Still, I used to be guilty of this fashion no-no: I once went to a flea market and bought dozens of fake designer pieces! What's worse, I totally pretended they were real!)

You just have to work your way up. If you want to wear designers, start with smaller pieces—buy a wallet for $300 by an amazing designer like Prada. (Their wallets are so chic and the leather is stunning—it's a great piece to start a collection.) Or tell Mom and Dad that all you want for Christmas is that one fabulous bag by Marc Jacobs, Gucci, or YSL. Start small and get that *one* thing that you can't live without. If you have an authentic, classic Louis Vuitton bag, that's something you can use all your life. (And when it's older, it's vintage and worth the same amount of money—maybe even more!) So if you do have a classic designer piece, keep it in good condition and hang on to it, lady! But don't waste your time or money unless it's the real thing.

FEARLESS TIP:

It's better to have one amazing real piece that will last forever than a thousand fakes, no matter how authentic they may look.

Don't: Buy Without Trying

It can be tempting to dash into a store, pick out some delicious-looking clothes, and be on your way, but then you miss out on one of the best parts of shopping—the therapy of it all! There's no greater escape from your everyday problems than flicking through racks of gorgeous clothing and trying everything on. Plus, if you don't try them on, you'll risk buying things that look good on the hanger but a hot mess* on you.

Fearless (Celebrity!) Tip

"When you're shopping for pieces that really work for you, my refrain is: 'Try it on, try it on, try it on.' Look at yourself in a three-way mirror and don't just try on a single piece. Try it on with items that you would wear it with so you get a sense of the proportion. If you're trying on pants, wear them with the heel that you would be wearing outside of the store."

—TIM GUNN

Do: Personalize Your Clothes

Whether or not you're a budding designer, there are things you can do to personalize your clothes to make them look great on you—or even one-of-a-kind.

First off, find a good tailor in your area. There's nothing worse than ill-fitting clothes. (Believe me, I know—I swam in my shirts as a teenager before I found the brands that were cut small!) Finding a good tailor is especially important for people with unusual proportions or sizes. I was so small as a teenager that even the tiniest size at Banana Republic didn't work for me, so a tailor would be the only way to fix it. If you're five foot two and all your jeans pool on the floor around your shoes, a tailor can do a quick hem job so you won't be folding your jeans up to keep them from dragging—not the cutest look.

When it comes to small fixes—like hemming and taking in—it can also be fun to learn a few tricks of the trade yourself. I learned to sew from watching my mom, but you can always look up this stuff online, too. You'll look much better in your clothes if you can do some simple tailoring to help them fit you better.

FEARLESS TIP:* *With the exception of celebrities and the superrich, who get their clothes custom-made, everyone buys clothes off the rack. So to make a great piece of clothing look even better, try personalizing it.

For those budding designers and artistic types out there, you can play around with unconventional alterations to personalize your clothes: When I worked at Bubbles in high school, I would rip up T-shirts and safety-pin them together. And I'd think, "Wow, I'm a fashion designer!" Of course, I was probably just a hot tranny mess,* but that's beside the point when you're playing around with fashion and personalizing. No one's judging you, so just have fun with it! Take a T-shirt and cut it into a tank top or a halter top. Or go to fabric stores, find trims that you love, and sew them onto the necklines of your camis. If personalizing your clothes is just a hobby, that's great—you'll stand out in what you're wearing. And if it sparks an interest in design, well, you know I think *that's* fabulous!

Do: What Makes You Comfortable—Just Don't Get Stuck

Make no mistake: You don't have to dress like I did back at Bubbles to be fierce and fabulous. But even if you prefer a classic look, take *some* chances with the way you dress. Accessorize your trouser jeans and plain top with a pair of crazy earrings or a fun, embellished bag (think a simple brown or black leather bag with studs or braiding detail on the handle, or maybe a patent leather bag with metallic detail). Say you wear a wide-legged pant most days of the week—try pairing it with a simple white button-down collared shirt. Then tuck it in, wear a fun belt, a great heel, and pull your hair back in a cute little bun. There are just so many ways to chic up a classic look so that it doesn't look boring. Some of the most fabulous people wear the most classic clothes. I would cheer for a woman in a black power suit every day—as long as she has the most amazing earrings in a fun shape with colored stones, and those flawless* five-inch Christian Louboutin heels on. It's so important not to get stuck in a rut—mix it up when you can and don't be afraid to step outside your comfort zone from time to time.

FEARLESS TIP:* *Remember—style isn't always about being eccentric or crazy.

EASY WAYS TO FAB UP YOUR OUTFIT

If you like to wear . . .	*then try adding . . .*
jeans	a pair of sleek high heels
T-shirts	fun jewelry, like a pile of necklaces or an armful of bangles
vests	a gorgeous pin or two
neutrals	a splash of bold color—in your shoes, accessories, or makeup
suits	a feminine handbag
button-down shirts	big, beautiful earrings

Fearless (Celebrity!) Tips

"Dress your age and make sure you are both stylish *and* comfortable."

—NIKI TAYLOR

"In fashion, I feel you have to experiment. I think most women, and that includes myself, can get very comfortable with one set of rules for the way we dress. Sometimes it is about trying things on and looking at things differently. And you'd be surprised; it gets very good results! I think it's about mixing and matching and breaking all those rules. Even if you are a very edgy girl, maybe you try something classic or try mixing the looks. I'm all about that mix and being experimental in terms of fashion."

—NINA GARCIA

Don't: Repeat a Full Outfit

will say this: No matter what fashion or financial!) stage I was in, I've never epeated a full outfit. And you don't have o have an endless closet to do it. You're going to repeat pieces, sure, but always nix it up. Add a new accessory, or wear our favorite top with a different bottom. But repeating a full, head-to-toe outfit is a no-no, if you can possibly help it.

FEARLESS TIP:

Repeating a full outfit means missing a chance to try wearing something new. Always change up at least one element of your outfit so you don't get stuck in a rut.

Do: Dress for Your Shape

t sounds obvious, but there are so many people out there who dress in clothes they love—but that don't necessarily work for them. Working *with* your shape, not against it, will have you looking great. Clothes that don't suit you are distracting (we've all seen those women in jeans two sizes too small!), while clothes that work with your shape will enhance your appearance. If you don't have the shape to pull off a pair of high-waisted skinny pants, don't buy them—you'll look much better in something that flatters you, and that's always more important than buying clothes based on how they look in a store window.

If You Have . . .

A large bust and a smaller lower half . . .

Try low-waisted skirts and pants. This will elongate you on top. Wear tops that come below your waistline to give you a more balanced shape. And accentuating your slim legs with a really tight legging or a skinny jean will elongate your entire body.

Avoid empire waists and high-waisted pencil skirts, which will make your bust look larger—and like it's sitting on a shelf. Not cute, trannies!*

A small bust and a larger lower half . . .

Try A-line skirts and fitted little blouses. Show off your top half in little tanks and camis. High-waisted, wide-leg pants will work for you, too.

Avoid form-fitting dresses, skinny jeans, and pencil skirts—they'll just accentuate the imbalance between your top and bottom half.

Fearless (Celebrity!) Tip

"I find that most people wear clothes that are either too big or too small for them, the more frequent error being too big. And it has to do with the comfort trap. It's really important to wear clothes that follow your own silhouette and that are formfitting. I'm not talking about wearing a scuba suit, but a lot of young women in particular wear clothes that have a lot of volume. I believe that part of what they're thinking is that the volume is disguising things that they may not be so proud of—a thicker midriff or a wide hip. In fact, it makes them look bigger. So you'll look slimmer if you wear clothes that follow your own silhouette."

—TIM GUNN

Curves . . .

Try simple pencil skirts and formfitting dresses if you want to accentuate curves. If you want to downplay your curves, a wrap dress that isn't supershort will elongate your body—and a pair of heels will do so even more because that extra height (and the good posture that comes with heels) always makes you look more long and lean. Also, a fitted long coat with a tie belt can really shape your body.

Avoid really cropped jackets or cropped pants. You don't want to break up the body if you're curvy. And be careful with your prints—small prints like little plaids can be cute, but a really wide funky plaid on a dress can be unflattering.

Few curves . . .

Try skirts that have pleating on the waist or hips, which adds shape. Or a piece with volume on top, like a poufy sleeve or a ruffled blouse. And a cropped bolero jacket adds variations in your body. Or add a great belt or a funky, cropped boot to your outfit—it will break up your body a little bit, which is something that works only with your shape.

Avoid straight looks that don't give you any added shape—you don't want to wear the skinniest pair of jeans you can find with a skin-tight T-shirt because you'll look like a stick figure! Don't forget to add that extra layer or cropped dimension to break up your body.

Fearless (Celebrity!) Tip

"I celebrate the wonders of belting long tops and dresses, which cinches the waist. Providing you have an hourglass of any kind, a belt can be a great enhancement. And if you don't have an hourglass, if you're straight or you're a little pear-shaped, having a belt that's slouchy—one that drapes from the hip bones—can be very, very flattering because it gives you an additional proportion. And I find, invariably, that it works for all sorts of body types. The belt can be wide, it can be thin, as long as it's what works best on you."

—TIM GUNN

Fearless (Celebrity!) Tip

"My most important fashion tip is to know your body. Knowing how you're built helps take the guesswork out about what will look good on you. Then, know your fabrics. Knits are always a go for my curves. And bias-cut gowns are fab for draping over curves as well."

—VANESSA WILLIAMS

Do: Love Your Hair

Now that you know the dos and don'ts of clothing, don't forget another important piece of your look: your hair. It really is one of the most important places to spend your time and money. Think about it. You are forced to look at your hair all day, every day. Every time you're in the bathroom, every time you pass a mirror. If you hate it, you're not going to look, feel, or act fierce.* If you like what you've got naturally, then work it out, honey, and more power to you! But if you aren't happy with your hair, don't be afraid to make a change.

Christian's Hair Affair

My natural hair is not cute. First off, it's curly (I'm Italian, lady!),* but not in a gorgeous, Rebecca Gayheart kind of way. It's frizzy and coarse and dry. And it's been a long and bumpy road to get it to look the way it does today. In junior high, I parted it straight down the middle—very Alfalfa from *The Little Rascals*, but wavy. Hot mess! A few years after that, I started using crazy amounts of gel and flattening my hair straight down on my forehead like Justin Timberlake in his 'N Sync period. (*That* was an abomination!) Next up? The Mohawk. My hair was huge and I shaved my head on both sides—the whole nine yards. It looked like a giant bird. It was around that time that I started getting my hair professionally straightened. Every week I'd get it chemically relaxed, and let me tell you, it *burned.* I would actually cry! But I could not stand my naturally curly hair. I would scream during the straightening, and it left my hair completely dead. But it was going to be *straight* if it killed me!

You don't have to go quite that far, of course, but you should experiment with your hair. Talk to stylists and find something that works for you; otherwise, you'll wake up every morning at a big deficit, since no outfit looks fabulous when you're hating your hair. Luckily, I discovered variations of my current style, my "fashion hawk," and I'm finally happy with it. I've even got the flat-ironing and styling down to a twenty-minute science!

Now that you're finding your own style and adhering to the dos and don'ts, you're ready to really personalize your own look. A great way to do that is to pick something to wear every day and make it your signature piece. Having a signature firms up your look and makes it distinctly *you.* Your signature can be anything as long as you wear it, wear it, wear it. Ever see a piece of clothing in a store and think, "Wow, that is *so* something that my friend Sarah would wear"? That's because your friend Sarah has a signature. And you can, too. Your signature piece should be something that you love so much that you want to wear it every day.

So how do you find a signature? I'd recommend picking something that you already wear often. Again, it can be anything (a hairstyle, à la yours truly; an armful of bangles, etc.), but here are some ideas that anyone can try out.

Skirts

If you love 'em, they might make a good signature for you. You're the girl who *always* wears skirts. No pants, no dresses. Want to try it? Start out by buying a variety of skirts, for instance, a classic black pencil skirt in lightweight wool, a printed A-line skirt, and a solid A-line skirt in a neutral color—gray is always nice. (Stay away from miniskirts, though. Your signature should be something you can always wear, and minis just aren't appropriate most of the time!) Shoot for buying at least five skirts from specialty stores like H&M, Zara, 3.1 Phillip Lim, Tory Burch, Banana Republic, bebe, Ann Taylor, or Club Monaco. Stick to a midprice range ($50–$200). Then just wear a skirt every day—Monday through Friday, at least. And mix up what you wear it with: Try pairing your skirts with flats, pumps, sweaters, blouses, and layered tops. It doesn't matter how you wear your skirts, just keep wearing them. That way, you're making the look your own and establishing your own signature.

FEARLESS TIP: Finding and wearing a signature piece all the time will take your look to the next level and really personalize your style.

Dresses

The same goes for dresses as for skirts—pick up a variety, maybe more like seven to ten (since you can't pair a dress with a second piece the way you can with a skirt). Where to buy: Banana, Gap, Ann Taylor, Club Monaco, and J.Crew. Department stores, too: I recommend going to Bloomingdale's and trying on designers like Diane von Furstenberg, BCBG, or Marc by Marc Jacobs. You've got a lot of room to play with dresses: Try prints, solids, long dresses, shorter dresses—whatever works for you. But every woman should have a classic, slim-fitting black dress. It takes off five pounds! Pick one that's simple with an easy neckline (V-neck or scoop) or something with more detail, like a trim at the shoulder. My favorite length hits right above the knee—it's flattering on most women in all different shapes and sizes. Another must is the shirtdress—they're cute and fun but still sexy (show a little leg in your shirtdress!). For the rest of your new dress collection, experiment with wrap dresses, sundresses, and prints—don't be afraid to ask salesclerks for their advice. And be sure to mix it up with your footwear and accessories. If you wear your classic black dress twice in one month, slick your hair back into a neat bun one day, and add a little cardigan, a string of pearls, and sleek black pumps. Then the next time you wear it, wear your hair down, add a pair of red flats, and add a patent leather black clutch. If dresses are your signature, then they're the common denominator—you're the girl who always wears dresses—but you keep it interesting by changing the other pieces of your outfit around it.

One Color

Another fun way to develop a signature is to pick one particular color that you love and wear it every day—whether it's a top or bottom in that color, or just a touch of it, like in your accessories. But it's important not to go over the top. If you love purple, that does not mean you should wear a purple dress and purple shoes, and carry a purple bag! Instead, wear a black dress with a purple shoe, and/or a fun earring that has a purple stone in it. The possibilities are endless when it comes to making a color your staple. If purple is your color, look for purple trims (like a black bag with purple piping, or a gray coat with purple buttons), printed tops with purple in the print, a pair of dark purple strappy sandals, a bracelet with purple beads, etc. And you can mix up the shade depending on the season—lighter shades like soft violet are great for spring whereas a darker shade, like eggplant or plum, works better for fall. Just remember not to go overboard—don't wear more than one piece (or two, max) with your color at a time—but *do* wear it every day. You're the girl who wears purple! That's fabulous!

Heels

For some women, wearing high heels *all* the time can be a fun wardrobe signature. If you want to make it yours, invest in as many as you can afford (five pairs, minimum, so you don't wear 'em out too fast, and so you can stock up on a variety of colors and styles that will go with anything in your closet). If you want to splurge, hit up Bloomingdale's or Saks, in store or online, for a fabulous stiletto heel by Christian Louboutin (the best of the best). In a more moderate price range, Steve Madden is great, as are Nine West and Bakers. Be sure to get a classic black pump, with a heel as high as you can handle (two to five inches). Every woman needs one. It can be any shape: pointy-toed, round-toed, or peep-toed. I also love a crazy-colored pump that makes a simple, classic outfit feel more fun and new. Red and purple always work. You should also have a pair of wedges—they're modern and easy to walk in. Always a plus!

My sister Shannon (who is really fierce,* by the way—much more on her later!) made heels her signature starting in middle school. She would wear stilettos or platforms every single day. It was amazing! She has hundreds and hundreds of pairs of shoes, and that's always been her thing. It's also many an icon's thing (hello, Imelda Marcos!) but it can be yours, too.

One Particular, Spectacular Accessory

Let's say you have an amazing necklace that you never take off. That can be your signature. Or an ornate, gorgeous cocktail ring (that would be fabulous!).

I had one spectacular piece as my signature for a while: my brown-and-white pony-skin cowboy boots, aka "the Ponies," by Donald J. Pliner. You may remember the Ponies from *Project Runway*—they are the most amazing thing in life and the high point of fierceness. I found them in a store in Baltimore when I was sixteen and I could have cried, they were so fabulous. A small fortune, too, at $600, but I was working two jobs at Bubbles and Banana Republic, so I went for it. And they paid for themselves: in the Ponies' heyday (they're retired now!) I wore them every single day, no matter what else I had on. Fabulous!

If shoes aren't your thing, you can make jewelry your signature. I had a phase a while back where I liked to wear tons of necklaces and Vivienne Westwood chains—like twenty of them! A great pair of earrings can really make any look and if you love them, then make wearing big earrings every single day your signature. There are a million places to pick up modestly priced jewelry—just make sure it's sterling silver or gold plated if you want to get mileage out of your pieces (though it's okay to throw in a few colorful, wear-'em-once cheapies for fun). And I'm all about rings. *Love* a big rock (and if it's real, even better!), so you can make rings your signature as well. Or you could just go off the deep end, be very avant-garde, and have your signature be *tons* of jewelry: a big bracelet, bangles, rings, earrings, or piles of necklaces. And when you're that adorned in jewels, you can just wear a T-shirt and still be fabulous!

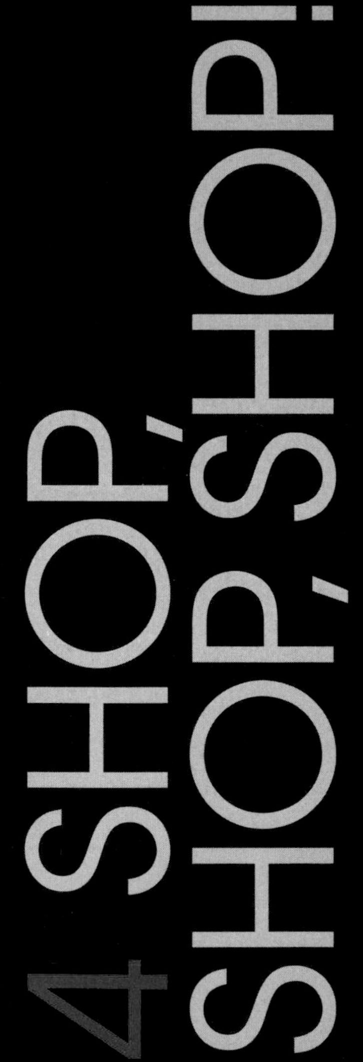

Have an idea for your look yet? Know what to do and what not to do? Then you, my dear, are ready to hit the stores—as a _fierce_* shopper, that is.

Build Your Basics

(***IMPORTANT NOTE:*** The stores I'll be naming here aren't the be-all and end-all of shopping. I picked them because they're all over the country, so no matter where you live you can build your own fierce style. But don't forget to hit up the cool smaller stores in different cities for extraspecial finds. I love stores like Intermix and Opening Ceremony—located in New York City and L.A.—where you can find cool European lines. Always be on the lookout for fun, unusual boutiques in your travels!)

Stock Up

Figure out what basics regularly go into your look (whether it's jeans, cardigans, hoop earrings, or tailored jackets) and which ones you feel good wearing. Then stock up on them. This way, you won't be agonizing in front of your closet every morning about what to wear!

Your own personal basics will depend on what you've discovered at this point. If you've done your homework (Ha! Listen to me, I'm like a professor of *fabulous*!*) and you've been thinking about what you love and what pieces you're already wearing regularly, reading fashion magazines, talking to people about their clothes, and checking out what's in the stores, then you should have a good idea of what your basics should be. Try to identify a certain kind of top, bottom, shoe, and accessory, and stock up. (See pages 65–70 for where to buy 'em!)

My basics include T-shirts from American Apparel or Uniqlo, skinny jeans, and funky sneakers in gold or patent leather. That's pretty much my uniform, so I've got several of each. If you love pencil skirts and button-down tops, buy a few of each. The more you have, the easier your morning routine will be—and you'll still look fabulous and put together.

Keep in mind that your basics will change over time. When I lived in London, my basics were pointy-toed boots, weird pants, and black turtleneck sweaters. All the time! So remember that fashion is an evolution, and your basics can (and usually, they should) change from time to time.

Accessory Basics

Don't forget about your accessories when it comes to the basics. I love when a woman has an oversized bag for day-time. Stock up on a few of those: one in black, since it goes with everything; a second in chocolate brown; and maybe a third in a bright, fun color like royal blue to spice up an other-wise ordinary outfit. You can have jewelry basics, too, like a certain style of earring or bracelet that you love. I'd recommend snapping up simple gold and silver necklaces with a single stone, bangles, and a chunky ring in any material. If you've got the basic cloth-ing pieces and the accessories, then you're all set for the day, with minimal planning. Once I've gotten dressed, I add cool sneakers like my black-and-gold patent pair, a black patent-leather belt, a big, crazy watch, and a fabulous bag, and I'm out the door!

Fearless (Celebrity!) Tip

"I have three fashion tips. Your first instinct is often right. Don't buy them if they are too high to wear. And always buy the correct size."

—WHOOPI GOLDBERG

Buy One Amazing Item

Now that you've got the basics, shift your focus to that high-impact piece. It can be a designer stiletto; an amazing-looking bag with great hardware or details; or a fabulous wrap dress in a chic print that totally flatters you and makes a statement. Whatever it is, wearing that one great, standout item makes your whole outfit better.

FEARLESS TIP:* *Wearing one great, standout, fabulous piece ups everything else.

Think about it like this: You're having a blah sort of day, just going through the motions at work without much excitement. But then you get a phone call from a friend with some fun weekend plans for you, and suddenly your whole day becomes a lot better. It's the same way with clothes. If someone looks a little frumpy in khakis and a dress shirt but she's carrying a unique and beautiful Marni bag, I would still think she looks fabulous!

Your one amazing piece can be anything, but if you're going to invest, I'd say go for a high-quality leather designer bag. One of the reasons designers make accessories (other than for their sheer fabulousness) is to reach the people who can't buy into a whole lifestyle brand but still want that luxury. Why a bag? You can wear it *everywhere.* I don't care where you're going. It can be the biggest bag in the world and you're going to the grocery store. And that's even more fabulous.

So when you're out looking for one, try to strike a balance between the crazy and the classic. You don't need to buy the embellished snakeskin bag for $10,000, but you also don't want to go too plain. Kooba bags, for example, are great because they come in neutrals like black or khaki, but they still look cool and fabulous. Gustto bags do, too, with their unique hardware. And if you're really splurging, go for an Yves Saint Laurent, a Lanvin, or a

Marni bag because they're also fairly neutral (but fabulous look-ing) and they'll go with everything.

Speaking of, that fabulous bag also needs to accommodate all the stuff you carry around with you (your day bag, that is—for evening, rock that teeny clutch all you want, lady!). I know I'd be lost without everything I take with me to be fabulous . . .

CHRISTIAN'S DAILY BAG MUST-HAVES

- *Cell phone*
- *Wallet*
- *Oversized planner (Being late is never fabulous.)*
- *A can of hair spray (Hey, sometimes it's necessary.)*
- *Bronzer (Because you never know where your day is going to take you!)*

Designer Lite

If you're working at Starbucks and Dior is totally out of the question, or you're on a budget that doesn't allow you anywhere near Fifth Avenue, you should know that many of the high-end designers have diffusion brands: Marc Jacobs has Marc by Marc Jacobs while Stella McCartney's got her Stella McCartney for Adidas line. Without going broke, you can still buy a great designer item.

CVS Chap·Block
SPACE
ENTER
TEXT
aircontrol
COBALT
15 PIECES SUGARFREE GUM

Top 10 Dream Pieces

Most people can probably afford one amazing piece—if they're lucky. But just for the fun of it, and in case you get really rich and famous one day and can buy whatever you want, here are my suggestions for dream items that every woman—and for most pieces, every man!—should aspire to own. (If you can't wait to own something off the dream list and need something like it right now, check out the "reality" pieces that follow each one!)

1 ***Burberry trench coat—classic and flawless.**** (Reality piece: a Banana Republic trench. It's the most bang for your buck: quality fabric, great hardware, and the fit is fabulous.)

Fearless (Celebrity!) Tip

"My favorite item in my closet is a long, chocolate-brown Burberry shearling coat I got as a Christmas present about five years ago. The outside looks rugged and beat up, and the inside is curly naturalness. It is the warmest piece of clothing I own."

—VANESSA WILLIAMS

2 ***A big, fun Marc Jacobs bag.*** (Reality piece: a designer bag from bluefly.com—they have a great selection in unique colors and shapes for $300 and under. I like Kooba, L.A.M.B., and Michael Kors.)

3 ***A classic black leather bag by Yves Saint Laurent.*** (Reality piece: a classic black bag from Club Monaco that won't come and go with trends and will always be stylish.)

4 ***A Marni accessory.*** Pick either a cuff bracelet in one of their weird fabrics or a pair of their futuristic earrings. It's almost costume jewelry, but the shapes are special (Reality piece: Aldo jewelry—love their fun use of trend accessories with feathers, studs, lace, and chains.)

5 ***Edgy heels by Alexander McQueen, Vivienne Westwood, Marni, or Proenza Schouler.*** (Reality piece: similar-looking heels at Aldo; they all end up reincarnated there a year later.)

Fearless (Celebrity!) Tip

"The most fabulous items in my closet are my Christian Louboutin heels—there are several pairs! I'm in love with that red sole and the high stiletto heel. Sometimes I see women pushing the sexuality too far. Things are too tight, too short. You really don't need to be so obvious when you want to capture a man's attention. When you have the cleavage, the short skirt, and the stiletto heels, you don't need *all* that. A subtle hint, like just the stilettos, works more effectively than such direct information."

—NINA GARCIA

6 ***Classic stiletto heels by Louboutin, Manolo, or Jimmy Choo.*** (Reality piece: Kenneth Cole classic heels in the $150–$300 price range.)

7 ***Chloé boots. A chunky Chloé boot for winter is perfection.*** (Reality piece: Steve Madden boots—they are always funky and on trend.)

8 ***A Prada suitcase (and a Prada makeup bag!).*** (Reality piece: designer luggage—Ralph Lauren is my fave—one season later at Marshalls or TJ Maxx.)

9 ***A pair of classic black Wolford tights.*** (Reality piece: basic black American Apparel tights.)

10 ***A Diane von Furstenberg wrap dress—preferably a print.*** (Reality piece: It's worth spending a few hundred dollars on this one.)

(That's right, divas, there's too much fabulousness for just 10 items . . .)

11 ***A cool rocker jean by Diesel.*** (Reality piece: jeans from Levi's, Forever 21, or Express—they have a great fit.)

12 ***A Chanel suit. Perfection!*** (Reality piece: suits are hard, so stick with department stores—and a helpful salesclerk—for that look.)

CHRISTIAN V SIRIANO

13 ***Louis Vuitton wallet in classic perfect brown.*** (Reality piece: Marc by Marc wallets are cute and cool! Other great bargain wallets: Kenneth Cole, Michael Kors, and Ralph Lauren.)

14 ***A Christian Siriano ruffled dress!*** Hello, I should be in here! (No substitute.)

Looking Fierce on a Budget

Whether or not you can afford to buy something (or everything!) off the dream list, you can still look fabulous without breaking the bank. Here are some of my favorite affordable places to shop and what you should buy there . . .

FEARLESS TIP: ***You can always rock fierce, inexpensive clothes without looking cheap.***

H&M

Go to H&M for basics and accessories—stockings, jewelry, and scarves. They're $3.99! The underwear, socks, bags, and sunglasses are also good to scoop up—cute and cheap. Some of the hats in my Fall 2008 collection for *Project Runway* were from H&M,

and I altered them to be extrafabulous. And the exclusive limited-edition lines by designers like Stella McCartney or Roberto Cavalli that crop up from time to time are no-brainer buys.

Target

This monster-sized superstore can be a hidden gem when a designer does a line for them. Even Park Avenue princesses go to Target to buy some designer lines! (The Proenza Schouler collection for Target was perfection.) It's a great place to stock up on basics, too. They have nice camis and T-shirts in all different shapes and colors that are perfect for layering under a suit or blouse. And like H&M, it's a good place to pick up socks, underwear, sunglasses, and the like. Anything that you want to buy cute and cheap!

Zara

Zara is a great lower-end brand and comparable to H&M. You pay a little more but you get the quality of an Italian company. If you're going to buy a piece that you want to last longer than one season, say a black trench coat, opt for Zara. The attention to detail in their clothes is amazing; they really follow trends, and the prints are always in sync with designer lines. (Some of my favorite shoes are from the Zara on Broadway in New York City—that's my little secret!)

Payless

If you need an inexpensive shoe fix, Payless is a great option, since their shoes are great quality, trendy, and cute. And I love that they can create a full look for you (shoes *and* accessories) for under $100. The designer collections (like Abaeté, Leila Rose, Patricia Field—and Christian Siriano, of course!) have been stunning, and with their price point you can walk away with five pairs of shoes for under $150! It really can't get better than that.

Nine West

I love a Nine West shoe. The look is a little older than Bakers but still fabulous, trendy, and cute. They follow the trends that are in stores in a given season and use fun materials like patent leathers and bright colors. And since they're not quite as tall, you'll still be able to walk in them! Heel height is really important. I love a huge heel, but I know it's not practical for everyday. Try a moderate heel size and stick with it (but break out those supermodel-tall heels for special occasions!).

Steve Madden

Steve Madden shoes are totally cute and up-to-the minute, so you can get a taste of what's popular in a given season and still have money for next year. Sometimes they can actually be too trendy (i.e., you won't be wearing them beyond their five minutes of fame), but they're still fun if the price is right. Steve Madden boots and booties are always on point.* The leather is quality and comes in fun colors like purple, yellow, and red; and the shapes are always new and exciting.

Department Store Shoe Sales

You can buy the most flawless shoes at a discount at Barneys and Bergdorf Goodman. You might find a ridiculous pair of Louboutins on sale! You may spend $200–$400 (instead of $50–$150 at one of the stores listed above), but you get the quality and the fabulousness of slipping your feet into *Louboutins.* Hello! That is something you want to cry about.

Other major department stores are worth checking out for their shoe sales, as well. You can find Saks, Nordstrom, and Bloomingdale's in many cities, and no matter where you live you can always shop online. And the sales happen all the time: when seasons change, during holidays, and at other random times, too. Check up on the Web sites every week or two to stay informed.

And when you're shopping the sales, if you see a fabulous pair of shoes that you love, even if they are from a few seasons ago, *buy them.* You'll have an amazing shoe, and it really won't matter when it hit the stores. If something is recognizable by season, like the sideways heel Marc Jacobs did a few seasons ago, you can always pass it off like you bought it when it first came out. Nobody knows when you bought that heel, so you wear it and be proud, lady!

Forever 21

This is where I go for great knockoffs. I look for coats—you can snag a detailed trench coat and not spend much money—skinny jeans, printed rocker T-shirts, and pencil and A-line skirts in gray and black. You'll get plenty of mileage out of them, and you can replace them next season if they're worn out. Tip: Go for black, white, and gray here. Stay away from the bright colors and prints (they look too cheap). The prices at 21 go from about $10 to $80—I never see anything over $100. Still, be a smart shopper and don't get those really wacky items. (No glitter tops!!)

Old Navy

Think more basic pieces here: tanks, skirts, and cute dresses. Steer clear of prints. Old Navy can be a good stop for summer: The flip-flops (if you *have* to do it) and the bathing suits are supercute—they both come in every color you can imagine, and the suits fit well. I also love that the size range is accurate—their XL really is an XL, and they offer a wide range of sizes.

If you're into prints, it's important to get the right ones. Go a little more high-end than your Gap and your Old Navy and hit up an Intermix or a Bloomingdale's. There, you're going to have more contemporary pieces like 3.1 Phillip Lim or Marc by Marc Jacobs that will, nine times out of ten, have nicer, more chic (and less cheesy!) prints.

Gap and Banana Republic

Gap has good-quality classic clothes in easy-to-wear materials. Banana Republic is one of my favorite stores of all time. Some of the best pieces come from the Republic! Their clothes range from low-end to fairly pricey. The designers who work for the brand really think about a person's lifestyle with their jewelry, hats, scarves, perfumes, holiday gifts—you name it, they have it. And their sales are absolutely unreal. You can get cute, high-quality shirts for $10 at Banana!

HOW TO SHOP SALES

Go in January. *Boutique and department-store employees always need a sale after Christmas, so they'll treat you like royalty—on top of selling you something fabulous at a discount!*

Get on mailing lists. *Whenever you find a store that you like, ask to be added to their mailing list. You'll be the first to know whey they're having a sale and be one step ahead of other shoppers. (Shopping as a competitive sport—I love it!)*

Don't obsess over sales. *If you do, you'll miss out on things. Lots of pieces don't ever get marked down and things sell out, so enjoy your sale shopping, but don't go crazy.*

High-End Fierceness

So for those of you who have the privilege of shopping high-end (and those of you who are splurging!) here a few tips on what's worth buying and where to get it.

Gowns and Cocktail Dresses

If you need to look truly fabulous for a special occasion, the dress is a great way to go all out. That's what people are really looking at when it comes to special occasions. If you can, go to Bergdorf's. They've simply got the best designer floor. Of course, there's only one Bergdorf's, so if you're anywhere other than New York, I also *love* Saks. They're all over the country and have a great selection online as well.

FEARLESS TIP:

There are certain key pieces in a wardrobe that are worth dropping serious dollar on if you have the means and the desire to do so. Just don't get carried away—focus your big spending where you will get the most out of it.

Shoes and Bags

As I'm sure you know by now, I am *all* about a great pair of heels and a fierce bag. But you should be, too, lady. The great shoes out there (Louboutin, Jimmy Choo, Manolo Blahnik) are made *so* well that your feet will survive the fabulousness and you'll be able to walk more than a block in them. Plus, those shoes scream luxury and style—it's a great way to make a statement. Same goes for bags (Louis Vuitton, Marc Jacobs, YSL, etc.).

Casual Wear

When it comes to casual wear, it *can* be worth it to spend a couple hundred dollars on something like a T-shirt if you're splurging. But do this only if you're buying something that's really innovative and different that not everyone else will be wearing. If it's supersoft and silky and there's something truly special about it, then go for it. Because when you buy a Lanvin tee for $300, you're buying more than just a top—you're buying the brand. Just be sure it looks cooler than its $13 counterpart at the Gap!

5 LEARN FROM THE PROS

Now that you've built a look and you're shopping your little heart out, you may want to look to the stars for guidance. No, not the ones in the sky, trannies,* the ones in Hollywood! The celebrities who have built fabulous* looks of their own can be some of the best people to learn from when it comes to looking fierce.* Like anything else you want to learn, it helps to look at the people who do it really well. Like in sports—if you're learning to ski, then why not watch the Winter Olympics on TV? You may be substituting bunny slopes for the giant slalom, but watching the people at the top can only make you better.

FEARLESS TIP: To look your fiercest, check out the people who do it well, and emulate them.

Watch the Best

Here are some of Hollywood's most fierce in fashion—watch them and learn . . .

Anna Wintour *(the mysterious icon)*

Vogue editor Anna Wintour truly has an endless closet. She could wear anything by any designer in the entire world! But even with infinite choices, she picks the trends best suited to her, and she always wears the most fabulous sunglasses. They work for her because they're signature Anna. (Remember my tip on page 40: Have a wardrobe signature!) It's probably a bit of strategy, too, since no one can tell what she's thinking about a fashion show. Is it fabulous? Is it a hot mess?* Who can tell behind those glasses?! Not only is she fierce, she's mysterious. It's *her* look and she rocks it constantly.

Anne Hathaway
(the quirky chameleon)

Anne is superelegant for her age, and she's totally old Hollywood. She reminds me of Jackie O. Totally gorg,* right? She could go to the Preakness in a giant hat, sunglasses, and pearls. But then the next day you could see her in a leather minidress! She's very classy, so she can pull off all sorts of different looks and it's never a trashy situation. I just love her—she's quirky in a way. Quirky elegant!

Vivienne Westwood (the individual)

Now *her* look is crazy! Vivienne wears all her own clothes: big muumuu-style, drapey, printed dresses and funky, high-heeled buckled boots, and her hair is dyed red-and-orange. So how does she manage to keep it fabulous when the same outfit would look a hot tranny mess* on someone else? Because (this is an important one, trannies, so take note) *all fashion depends on who's wearing it.* Some clothes wear the person and some people wear the clothes. Vivienne's been dressing this way since it was okay to wear crazy weird outfits back in the '60s and '70s (unlike today, when it's cool to hate on what people wear). I totally admire her.

Sarah Jessica Parker *(the fashion plate)*

SJP's über-fashionable character on *Sex and the City* has impacted her style—she has a little bit of that Carrie Bradshaw in her! Sarah Jessica dresses very fashion-forward. It's not always perfect, but it's perfect for her. She won't always wear the typical ball gown at the big events—she's a risk taker, which I *love.* That's what creates an icon and that's what creates fashion. If every designer and every celebrity decided to be safe in what they wore, then everybody would look the same. Thank God for Sarah Jessica Parker!

Fearless (Celebrity!) Tip

"I'm always talking about the semiology of clothes—they send a message about how we want to be perceived, and, ideally, that message should be who we are. It's a matter of what you do, with whom you interact, and how you want the world to perceive you. So it's critical that everyone embrace that first, and then figure out how to dress for that role. I think it's useful for young people in particular to have a fashion icon—someone whose style they have great regard for. And I also think it's important for one's icon to have a shape and proportions that are close to their own. Getting it right on you means making sure the silhouette, proportion, and fit all work on your body. So when you're looking at clothes on someone and you think, 'Oh, that looks great on her,' it doesn't necessarily mean it will look good on you. Luckily, you can see great style on all sorts of body types, whether it's Nikki Blonsky or one of the Olsen twins!"

—TIM GUNN

Victoria Beckham
(the risk taker)

If anyone is a true risk taker, it's Victoria Beckham. She wears the highest shoes you can make and she wears the biggest sunglasses you can buy and the tightest little dresses. But you know what? I don't think she really cares what people think of her. So she's the type of person that can set a trend—a sexy, sultry, diva trend. Sarah Jessica Parker and Victoria Beckham are total opposites style-wise, but they're both completely fabulous because they each have a daring look. They work it and they own it, and nothing is more fierce than that.

Halle Berry *(chic and sexy)*

Halle is simply stunning, and she'll always be an icon. She always manages to look chic and sexy at the same time, which is not an easy combination. (Pre-baby and post-baby, too—no matter her size, she always looks effortlessly fabulous.) So many women strive for her chic-sexy combination, and they should—look at Halle! She works those Grecian-style gowns with a sexiness that comes from within.

> ***Fearless (Celebrity!) Tip***
>
> **"The colors that Halle Berry wears really complement her skin. I love that."**
>
> **—MODEL SESSILEE LOPEZ**

Natalie Portman *(the artsy fashionista)*

Natalie Portman has been looking especially amazing lately, and she's wearing all the high-end designers. She doesn't care what the trend is, and she loves the artistic side of fashion. She's not the type to ask a designer to make her a dress. For her, it's "Make me a piece of art."

Debra Messing *(just glamour)*

I love Debra. She's got the best hair in Hollywood! Every time I see her on a red carpet she is one hundred percent *on point.** I think she is so super chic and that hair is always flawless.* The red locks are stunning! She always rocks the classic Hollywood glamour, but with the most fun and exciting personality. She's maybe not as funky as some of my other faves, but she embodies class and is truly chic.

Choose an Icon of Your Own

Now, think about all the well-known people whose style you admire. Whose closet would you absolutely love to raid? It can be anyone—an actor, a musician, even a politician—just as long as it's someone with a body type that's similar to yours, and someone who portrays an image like the one that you want to portray. Study their clothing and see if you can mimic the looks you love most.

6 CONCLUSION: DON'T BE BORING

I hope you've taken away some helpful tips about how to look fierce.* But as a final note on the matter, I hope you'll remember this: Wear what you love, take risks, try on trends, even embrace a crazy idea. Just don't be boring. That means not wearing the everyday, easy items (T-shirt, jeans, flip-flops) without injecting any of your personality. Clothes are boring when they don't express who you are. You could be the most fascinating, fun, *not*-boring person in the world, but your clothes need to reflect you—your personality, your loves, your inspirations. Take risks and take chances. You might not always get it right, but you'll always be interesting. And that's what fashion is all about, divas!*

And hopefully you're well on your way to developing your own look, hitting the shops, and holding fast to my dos and don'ts—maybe even coming up with some of your own. Because while I can guide you in the right direction (and let's face it, I *am* right most of the time—hello!), "fierce" is something we all need to define for ourselves. These are my own personal guidelines for how you can look fierce, but feel free to add on as you see fit. I think that's fabulous.

And now that you're looking great, it's time to move on to some equally important stuff: feeling and acting fierce. I think that the way you look can directly affect how you feel and act, so hopefully you're well on your way. Now put on those fabulous* heels and strap in for Part Two: We're working on the *inside* next, so your fierceness will shine through even brighter.

FEARLESS TIP:
You can never be fierce if you're boring. Find that look that's right for you and rock it out. It's the only way to look fierce.

Finding Your Inner Ferocia

Here's the deal. You can have all the right clothes in the world: your fabulous Marni bag, Louis Vuitton everything, perfect jeans, flawless heels in every color, and a closet for days. But if you don't *feel* as fierce as you look, well, then it all goes out the window, lady. Because your clothes, no matter how fabulous, are only on the outside. So what does it mean to feel fierce? When you feel fierce, you feel confident, proud, secure, and self-assured. And having those qualities is fabulous in a way that no piece of clothing will ever be—feeling fierce colors everything about you, and like a great accessory, it just makes everything you're wearing look better.

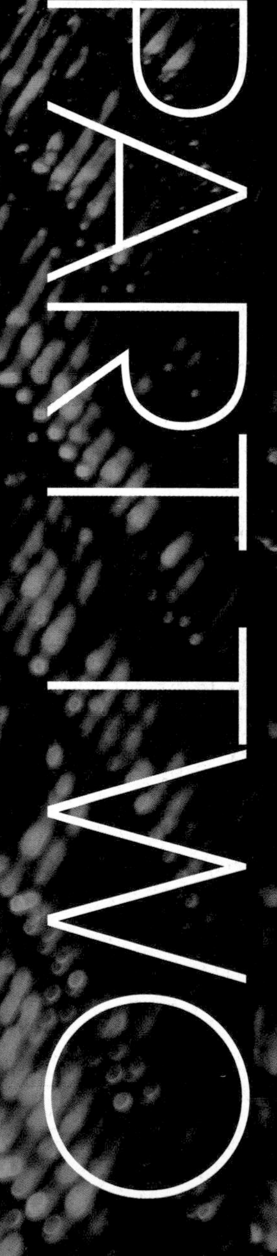

PART TWO

Ever since *Project Runway* people have been asking my friends, "Is Christian really like that?" And the answer, for the most part, is yes! I've jokingly said "I'm kind of a big deal" for as long as I can remember, and when I was little I would actually tell people, "I'm really going to be famous one day." But part of me truly believed it. I always knew I'd be a fashion designer somehow. I know who I am, I own it, and most of the time I'm pretty darn happy with it. And the first step to feeling that way yourself means being *you,* through and through.

The way you feel about yourself is the most important element when it comes to feeling fierce.* You've got to feel great about who you are before you can put any kind of fabulousness* out there in the world. So, in your quest for fierceness, you've got to work on feeling good about what's inside—think about it as an inner makeover!

Don't Worry About What Anyone Else Thinks

If you're being true to yourself and loving the person you are, whatever you choose to do is gonna be fierce! Of course, this is easier said than done. (Hello, high school?!) It can take years to be comfortable enough with yourself not to care what others think. But when you do—even for a moment—you'll start to truly feel fierce. Maybe you love playing chess and you want to join the chess club at school, but that isn't a "cool" thing to do. Or maybe the way you like to dress turns heads in your office (and not in an "Ooh, love that, where did you get it?" sort of way). Whatever it is, if it makes *you* happy, it just doesn't matter what other people think.

Fearless (Celebrity!) Tip

"What makes me feel confident, fearless, and fabulous is knowing that I can be myself."

—WHOOPI GOLDBERG

Learning from a Pro

I was lucky to learn this lesson early on, thanks to my sister Shannon, who was very eccentric in high school. She had hundreds of stiletto and platform heels and wore a different pair every single day, along with a crazy outfit—sometimes she'd actually wear a costume to school! So her style was pretty offbeat, and I'm sure people made fun of her. (Can you imagine a high school where a costume and high platform heels would blend in?) But it didn't stop her from doing it. And that's how I learned to do the same. Shannon was my hero, and whatever she did, I wanted to do, too.

FEARLESS TIP: Don't change what you're doing just to fit in with other people. If you do, you're only cheating yourself.

With Shannon as my role model, I was able to take risks at a very unforgiving time—my teenage years. As you know, I grew up in a preppy, nautical town where being a little conservative was the norm. But while working at Bubbles, I was wearing mesh shirts and sequined pants! And people made fun of me for it. I was five foot two, and crazy skinny with huge, spiky hair and outrageous clothes—it's a wonder I got out of there alive! But I honestly wasn't that concerned about what people thought or said about me. I could take those risks with my looks because Shannon always did, and I faced criticism as she would—staying true to myself and ignoring anyone who didn't like it. Regardless of what people thought or said about my sister, she was happy. So I did what made me happy, too.

And it went beyond just my wardrobe. After my freshman year of high school, I decided to apply to the Baltimore School for the Arts. The norm in high school, of course, is to play it safe and try to blend in, so it was a risk to leave my regular high school in favor of an art school—and it is something that very few kids do. But I thought that I could really be myself there and do what I loved, so I took a leap of faith and I went. It actually turned out that I was one of the most normal-looking people there! It was a place where I could wear and do pretty much whatever I wanted without the judgment I'd face in a regular school.

So whoever you want to be, be true to that person. If anyone has a problem with it, you can send 'em to me, lady!* But remember: Being true to yourself and feeling fierce about it doesn't necessarily mean being outrageous. You don't have to wear sequins or costumes like me and my sister to feel fierce. You just have to be you.

Fearless (Celebrity!) Tip

"I think no matter how 'fierce' your clothes are, a look still has to be you. If you're not comfortable or if something's not your style, it always shows. The opposite is true, too—if you're rocking an outfit you love, you'll feel confident, fearless, and fabulous no matter what anyone else thinks—there's nothing sexier than that!"

—HEIDI KLUM

Own It!

Once you're able to distance yourself from what other people think, it's time to work on developing pride and confidence in the choices you make for yourself. That means feeling confident about whatever you choose to do—even when you step out of the box and take risks. Because not everyone is going to like the way you look or the choices you make. But as far as I'm concerned, I'd much rather be interesting and do my own eccentric thing than just blend in with the masses.

FEARLESS TIP:

If you look or act like everyone else, then you're not going to be interesting. Part of being fierce is about truly owning who you are.

Owning It on the *Runway*

One of the most important times that I truly owned who I was happened at the end of *Project Runway*. When I knew I was going to Bryant Park for the finale, I wanted to win *so* bad. I could taste it, smell it, hear it—I had to win.

So I took who I am as a designer—I love drama and volume and edge in my clothes—and I *owned* that. *Everything* in my finale collection had flounce and ruffles and layers. I took great pride in

what I loved to do and did it in a big way. Instead of a safe, edited-down collection of wearable clothes, I made everything a little crazy: a feathered gown, an hombre flounce dress with a tightly cinched belt, a ruffled neck piece that covered my model's face! This went beyond not caring what people thought—this was about being me and putting it out there with confidence. *Owning it.*

Of course, this comes with a risk—people may not like what you put out there, no matter how much you own it. I knew that my decision to own my aesthetic and make a really out-there collection on *Runway* would result in one of two things: Either the judges would love that I owned who I was and truly worked my personality into the clothes, or . . . they'd hate it! But I think it's far better to have a strong point of view, own that, and flaunt it than to quiet your instincts and play it safe.

FOUR WAYS TO OWN IT

There are several ways to own who you are, both in terms of how you look and what you do. Here are some fun ones to try out . . .

1 *Wear a color that not everybody can wear. Pick a shade that flatters your skin tone and your eyes and makes* you *look gorgeous and fabulous. Maybe try wearing a fuchsia that not every person in the world is going to wear. Making it personal will make you* feel *fierce.*

2 *Take a class in something crazy. Like to dance? Then why not sign up for a class in African tribal dance or yoga ballet? If you're a dancer (even a new one), go out there and dance in every way you can.*

3 *Get some highlights that not everybody can pull off. Say you have the most gorgeous blonde hair and you want to be* really *blonde and fabulous. Well, not everyone can be really blonde and fabulous! Plenty of people just can't go there because they would look like a hot tranny mess.* A brunette girl who goes superfierce and fabulous blonde? She is* so *not the same as you, Ms. Blonde Ambition!*

4 *Flaunt your assets: If you have great legs and you can wear high-heeled shoes all day, wear 'em! Wear the craziest high heels every day. Throw a little Carrie Bradshaw (or Shannon Siriano!) in there, why not? This applies to other assets, too . . . Do you like to write? Then whip up a special speech the next time a friend gets married. Or put together a sweet little poem for a friend's birthday. Or even write up a witty toast for your next casual get-together.*

When you come up with something that only you *can do, that only* you *can pull off, you're going to feel fabulous, plain and simple. Look at me: Not everyone is going to be able to rock this fashion-hawk hairstyle or use crazy expressions like "hot tranny mess" like I do! These things are truly me—and I own them.*

Guilty Pleasures

In being true to yourself and owning who you are, it's important to embrace all of you—and that includes those cheesy, fun-loving aspects of your personality. I know I tend to condemn all things cheesy, but I think you should embrace those silly things that *you* love during your downtime. I always own my guilty pleasures, no matter what people may think! Many of them are silly, but they're me, and they make me feel good. And that's what feeling fierce is all about.

FEARLESS TIP:
Indulge yourself in whatever you love—no matter how silly it may seem.

So, for some inspiration—or maybe a few laughs—here are a whole lot of *my* favorite things. Some of them are in no way fabulous—but they're definitely still fierce. Try them out sometime, or indulge in your own!

MY FIERCE FAVORITE . . .

Food

Subway (I eat it practically every day!)

Yodels

McDonald's milkshakes

Hot Pockets! (I'm obsessed—I love microwaveable food. Is that bad?)

Frozen veggie burgers

Music

Christina Aguilera

Britney Spears

Mariah Carey

Rihanna

Cyndi Lauper (All my diva girls!)

Brad Walsh

Movies

Glitter (It's actually a good movie! I don't care what anyone says. It's all Mariah's music, so if you love that you'll love *Glitter.* Sure, it's cheesy, but something about it is pretty good. Kind of like Britney's *Crossroads*!)

Don't Tell Mom the Babysitter's Dead (My favorite, favorite, favorite movie growing up, other than *The Wizard of Oz,* of course. Until a few years ago, I didn't even remember that the main character in the movie was a fashion designer. Maybe that is why I got into design! After all, I *did* watch the movie every single day . . .)

Mrs. Doubtfire (Because Robin Williams dressed up in a costume, and I loved that!)

The Devil Wears Prada

Jurassic Park

The *Bourne* series (I like boy movies, too!)

TV Shows

Buffy the Vampire Slayer (Old school!)

Full House (Love!)

Step by Step

Family Matters (Really, I was obsessed with all of TGIF. And if you don't know what that means, then you're over. Expired.* I'm all about the old TV shows. They're vintage—still very cool.)

Saved by the Bell (That was my show!)

Sex and the City

The Biggest Loser (*So* good!)

Gossip Girl

The Rachel Zoe Project

Project Runway (Of course! I watched it all the time in London.)

Restaurants

Angelina's Café on the Lower East Side in Manhattan

The Chart House in Annapolis

Mangia's in Annapolis

T.G.I. Friday's (That's my jam.)

Pizza Express in London (Totally cheesy. Love that.)

Sea in Williamsburg, Brooklyn (Where I live!)

The cool Thai place *next to* Sea (In case you can't get in!)

Fabiane's Café and Pastry in Williamsburg

Drinks

Starbucks's Java Chip Frappucino

Stoli raspberry and Sprite (So gay!)

Any champagne cocktail with strawberries at Selfridges in London (They're like $17 a glass!)

Reading Material

Elle

Vogue

I.D. magazine (That's my favorite!)

Women's Wear Daily

Zink

Fierce Style by Christian Siriano!

Handling Criticism

So let's say that you're being true to yourself and owning who you are in every way. This is all totally fierce, trannies,* but just because you are feeling fierce about yourself doesn't mean everyone else will. No matter who you are or what you do, there will always be people who don't like the way you look, the way you act, or what you do. So the next stop in acquiring the fierceness is learning how to feel that way in the face of criticism.

FEARLESS TIP:* *Feeling fierce isn't about just being cool, confident, and good at what you do. Fierceness is also built from being tough and withstanding the critics.

Stay Tough!

There's no faster way to lose that fierce feeling than when you face criticism. But the bright side is that if you believe in what you're doing and you're able to persevere through a harsh critique, you'll find new strength in your skills and opinions. And while criticism is never fun, handling it will become easier the more you believe in yourself.

The Fashion Jungle

Let me tell you, working in fashion is not easy. In fact, it can be a total pain in the ass! People in the industry can be incredibly critical, even mean. Experiencing that didn't just toughen me up. It helped me to stay stronger in my own opinions. The fashion industry is difficult in a way that others aren't. In an office, for example, people gossip. They may say rude things behind one another's back. But in fashion, so many people are outspoken and opinionated that they just come right out with their critiques and opinions and say them to your face—nice or not! People have told me that my work is one-note, that I'm too over-the-top, unwearable—you name it, I've heard it. So I learned to have the same open, outspoken opinions about my work. If I think something that I did is fabulous and well-done, I tell myself (and others!) just that.

Fearless (Celebrity!) Tip

"People are so scared of being made fun of that they don't take risks. How can you be fabulous if you look just like everyone else? I once went to an event in an old '70s-style vintage dress that I had bought in the West Village in New York City. I felt amazing. Next day, I was on every worst-dressed list imaginable. Guess what? I would wear it again in a heartbeat."

—BECKI NEWTON

Have No Fear

If you haven't caught on thus far, I'm calling my tips "fearless" for a reason. You can't be scared of what critics might say about your new outfit, hobby, or anything else you do. Otherwise, what's the point in doing it in the first place?

FEARLESS TIP:

If you're gonna be fierce, you simply must be fearless—in fashion, in life, all the time.

They may sound alike, but "fear" and "fierce" have nothing to do with one another. In fact, I'd say fear is the complete opposite of fierce. Here's an example . . .

Going for Gold

Last year I went to the *Sex and the City* movie premiere (fabulous!) in New York City. I took my model friend Lisa Nargi, who wore a crazy red dress that I'd made for the occasion, and I wore a gold lamé shirt. As far as I'm concerned, you want people to remember what you wore to a big event. But then all these bloggers came out and said I looked like Liberace in my gold lamé! In the days that followed, people wrote terrible things about me, like:

"In case you forgot, he's supposed to be America's next great fashion designer."

"He's a pair of roller skates short of a party at Studio 54."

"His outfit was not a hot tranny mess—it was a flat-out disaster."

As you can see, the general consensus was that I looked pretty awful at the *Sex and the City* premiere. Now, I would be lying if I said I wasn't stung by these opinions—no one wants to hear that people hate how you look or that your peers are

making fun of you. I hate when bloggers write mean things! Who wouldn't?

But after those comments came out, the bad feelings didn't last long, and here's why: My outfit was flashy and edgy and totally risky, no doubt. But it was fun and it was different, and we were at a premiere for one of the most fashion-inspiring movies of the year! Why would you want to wear a suit or a boring outfit to a movie premiere that only a few select people go to—let alone for a movie defined by its style?!

Hurt feelings aside, here's the bottom line: People were blogging about me—and I loved it. They remembered me, and I don't care if it was because they hated my outfit. Whatever! No matter what you wear or what you choose to do, if it's right for you then anyone who criticizes you is just not as fabulous as you are. So do I have any regrets about wearing my panned *Sex and the City* outfit? *Hell* no. Wear gold. I think it's great. So great that I wore that very same top to the Emmy Awards that fall, trannies. Work.*

So no matter what you do, divas, do it without fear. Fear shuts you down, keeps you from taking risks, and keeps you from feeling fabulous.

8 FEEL GOOD ABOUT YOURSELF

Now that you're being true to who you are, it's time to really feel great about yourself. Let that Ferocia Coutura* shine through, lady! I think it's a shame that people often confuse this with arrogance. In fact, I think life would be really tough if you didn't feel good about you! One of the easiest ways to start feeling great about yourself is to find something that you can totally rock—and that is a huge part of feeling fierce. Straight out of Transylvania,* lady!

Develop Your Talents

So how do you become really good at something? Have a hobby that you enjoy? Wish that you did? Either way, it's key to build that up . . .

Find a Hobby

Don't have one special skill that you love to do? I'm sure there are plenty of people who would love to learn a new skill that they've never tried before.

So do it! Who's going to judge you? You're not on TV, and you're not going to be in the gossip magazines every day. You can do whatever you want!

That's an important lesson I've learned in the past couple years—if you're in the public eye, people are going to judge you, plain and simple. (Look at what happens when film actors try their hand at Broadway—the critics jump all over them. And can you imagine what would happen if Angelina Jolie decided to learn to surf? The paparazzi would

FEARLESS TIP: *You can't underestimate the confidence that comes from trying something new.*

be all over it!) Luckily, you don't have to worry about that. Always wanted to dance? Garden? Paint? Write romance novels? Whatever it is, nothing will make you feel more fierce and fabulous than discovering something new that you absolutely love to do.

Even if your new endeavor turns out to be a total failure after a week or so, you can ditch it and try something else. Take advantage of that freedom: As much as it feels like people are watching and judging you, they're really not. They're too busy wondering if *you* are judging *them*!

Let's say you want to learn how to sew, but there aren't any classes offered in your area. What do you do? Hello!? The Internet! It really is the most amazing way to learn a new skill. If you type "how to sew in a zipper" into Google, you can download a step-by-step guide with pictures. You can learn almost any sewing project that way. Sewing is very step-by-step, and if you pay attention to directions it can be totally easy and fabulous.* Say you make your own skirt and wear it to a party, and everybody compliments your fabulous skirt and asks where you got it. Then you can tell them, "I made it." You will get the most amazing compliments because it's *yours*. And it's one-of-a-kind! A *you* original. People are really impressed by that because it's such a craft and it's something that so many people don't do on their own.

Enhance Your Talents

Once you've found a new skill that you want to try, or an old hobby that you'd like to improve upon, see how far you can take it. Take that skill and really work it. You'll be feeling confident about yourself before you know it!

Say you're this amazing baker, and you make the most delicious cupcakes. Why not go to house parties in your neighborhood and bring the cupcakes along? If they're gorgeous and they taste fantastic and everyone wants them, you can't help but feel like, "Ooh, I'm fabulous, I make the best cupcakes." Doing something well leads to more confidence: If you feel great about the hobby you're pursuing, maybe next you'll want to *look* fabulous while you're doing it! So for all these cupcake parties you're throwing, you go out and buy the most amazing pair of shoes. And suddenly, you go from being just a casual baker to the fabulous woman who bakes the most amazing cupcakes and wears flawless* heels—and everyone will love both! More important, you will, too.

FEARLESS TIP: You'll build even more confidence if you're doing something well.

Let Others Push You

It can be helpful when someone around you is pursuing your hobby, too, because it pushes you to be even better at it. If you want to be great at something, there's nothing wrong with a little healthy competition—that's always fierce.* (After all, they do call it *fierce* competition! Hello!) Athletes are constantly competing against each other, each trying to be a little bit better than the others. So if everyone's competing, then everyone is going to keep getting better and better at what they do. Try recruiting a friend to pursue a hobby with you. If you're both into gardening, check out your friend's garden on occasion. Maybe she's got some big, fat, healthy tomatoes and all you have are herbs. Well, you'd better grow some fabulous vegetable, too, lady! It may sound silly, but no matter what you do, if you've got someone else urging you on, the result can be even more delicious.

Get to Work

Hobbies are a great way to feel good about yourself, but working can be even better. Having a job from an early age is a great way to build confidence and find yourself. Being responsible for something as a teenager made me take a lot of pride in what I was doing, and it made a big impact on who I am today. If you are enjoying your job—whether it's making cappuccinos, teaching summer camp, or doing hair, like I did—it can really help establish pride, ownership, and confidence. It's a shortcut to feeling fierce!

Bubbles Diva

I was just thirteen years old when I started working. I got a job at the Orange Julius juice stand at the Annapolis Mall. But while I was making smoothies all day, my attention was really focused on another mall destination—Bubbles salon. Every day from my juice stand I would see these *fabulous* girls and guys walking out of there. They had wild hair and tattoos and crazy outfits and it was like *The Wizard of Oz* all over again. I was mesmerized. They would always stop by Orange Julius, so we started chatting. Then one day, to my shock and awe, one of them casually said,

"You should come work with us." I quit my job on the spot. Forget showing at New York Fashion Week—in that moment, I had *made* it.

Bubbles is a chain made up of thirty to forty salons, and the one that I worked in was among the top locations in the entire company. It had the most traffic—and some of the best employees. I was working with stylists there who were making more than $200,000 a year doing hair. In Maryland! These were not stylists in New York City; they were not charging $300 for a haircut. The Bubbles stylists charged between $50 and $100, but that was a *lot* for that area.

So here I am at thirteen, and (brace yourself) a little conservative! I was wearing shirts buttoned all the way up and I was quiet and had *really* not-cute hair. (Remember the gelled abomination I described in Part One? So bad!) But all of the people at the salon were *such* characters—just what I wanted to be. In my first few weeks of working at Bubbles, all

the stylists were playfully pushing me around and being sassy and telling me what to do. And I was *not* having that! So even though I started out as the buttoned-up oddball, I changed that real quick. I started dressing more like them and trying to fit in with the group. Thinking back, they probably pushed me around like that to get me to loosen up. And hey, it worked! Pretty soon, I was among the cast of characters at Bubbles salon. Everyone was eccentric in their own way and I was thrilled to be one of them. I had found my place.

When I was starting to hit my stride at the salon, I had a moment where the confidence just clicked for me—I felt extremely comfortable with myself and what I'd learned. And that, in turn, made everyone really comfortable around me. It was almost like a weight had been lifted. When I started my job, I was a little insecure. I didn't look like my coworkers, and I wasn't sure I'd be as good as they were at the job. But once I started feeling confident, that freed me up for other pursuits—like making friends with those coworkers and looking as fabulous as they did! Pretty soon, I had a network of friends, and I began developing the personality and look I have today.

In a lot of ways, I really grew up at that salon. It was such a mix of people. There were fourteen- to sixteen-year-old receptionists who were in hair school part-time, and stylists who were in their thirties and forties, but in a way, all of us were on the same level. Nobody talked down to you if you were just a shampoo tech, because all the assistants and receptionists did so much work. And it was different from your average after-school job in that I was working with people for whom this was a career. So in a way, I had

to mature very quickly, because it wasn't just a little part-time job, like working at the Orange Julius or your local McDonald's.

What's more, it turned out that I really loved to do hair. So I took it very seriously. I think that was also how I got so comfortable with myself and with other people so quickly; in that environment, you have to hold your own and you have to be on the same level as your coworkers—even if you're fourteen and they're forty-five. So even though the atmosphere was fun and light (some of my words and catchphrases, like "Lady!"* come from the salon!), I took it very seriously. Looking back, I can see the sense of responsibility and accomplishment that I took away from that job. It set up the fierceness, trannies!*

Working It: Flaws and All

To truly feel good about yourself, you've got to do more than just rock out at your hobbies and your job. No one is good at everything they do. So to truly feel good about yourself and feel fierce, you have to find a way to accept your flaws. Everyone has something they don't like about themselves—but not everyone can put that aside, see beyond it, and work it out anyway. The people who can are the ones that truly *feel* fierce.

If you're uncomfortable with something that you're not so great at, or if something about the way you look is not going to change anytime soon, do your best to take your focus away from it. Maybe it's a bad review at work, trouble with your skin, or even your weight. Honey, I know plenty of women who aren't happy with their size, but they're still some of the most fabulous people you'll ever meet in your life. They rock their wardrobe, or their hair, or whatever they love about themselves, and shift the focus away from any self-perceived flaws. The same goes for work—maybe you're a teacher but the discipline aspect of your job is difficult for you. If that's the case, don't focus on what you perceive as a flaw. Instead, spotlight how great you are at helping your students understand tough concepts in class, and just do the best you can on the areas that are hard for you.

FEARLESS TIP:

Take your focus away from the negative and focus on what's positive and what's fabulous. The more you do that, the more fierce you will feel!

Skinny Minny

I've never been a big guy (shocker, right?), but when I was younger I was especially skinny. So shopping posed a real problem. A size Small in most stores wouldn't even fit me! So instead of dwelling on what I didn't like about my appearance, I learned to take the emphasis away from what I didn't love (my slight stature) and move it to something I did, like my hair! I did what I needed to do to deal with my flaw (buying pants from the women's section at Banana Republic, trannies!) and shifted the focus to my wacky hairstyles and to the unique personality I was developing. My body type wasn't going to change, so I took the focus off how skinny I was and turned it toward bigger things, like my big hair and my bigger personality!

Making Fierceness Happen

Contrary to what you might think, I don't flit through every day chanting "Faaaabulous" and attending parties without a care in the world. I do have my downtime. Like anyone else, I don't always feel good about myself. I get sad, even downright depressed, at times. But because I have big dreams, I look at the big picture so I can feel fierce through the tough times, too. No matter how much confidence you have, there are going to be times when things just don't feel fierce. You don't feel great about how you look, work isn't going well, or you're fighting with someone you love. So when that happens, here are some of the ways that I turn the mood around and feel fierce again . . .

FEARLESS TIP: Feeling fierce doesn't always just happen. Sometimes you need to work to feel that way. Luckily, there are some fun, fabulous ways to do just that.

Look Back on Your Accomplishments

Sometimes I'll go through old portfolios or old photos of work that I've made or articles that people have written about me. Everyone has done something great at one point in his or her life—so keep a reminder of it around. Maybe it's a project you did at school or work that you're really proud of. Even if it's something you did just for fun (a drawing, painting, or photograph, perhaps), you can't look back on it without smiling.

Be a Workaholic

When I have trouble feeling fierce, it helps me to work really hard on whatever project I have at the moment. For those diva students out there, don't underestimate the confidence that comes with working on a paper, a project, or a test that goes really well. I guarantee that will make you feel amazing.

Indulge in Retail Therapy

Need to get out of the house to improve your mood? Then another great pick-me-up option is . . . wait for it . . . shopping! I always think that it's the best therapy. I love to just walk around and people-watch. You don't even have to buy anything; sometimes just window-shopping does the trick! When you have those down days, go out and just do something. It helps to be around people who are in a better, more fabulous state of mind.

Make Someone's Day

Send voice mails and text messages to your loved ones. When I sleep in on a weekend day, then wake up and see that I have missed calls and texts from my friends saying, "How are you? Miss you! Love you!" it gives me a great feeling. So spread that fierceness around, and send a random text message or e-mail to someone you love to make them feel fabulous, too!

Need other quick, fierce fixes and instant gratifications?

FIVE MORE QUICK AND EASY WAYS TO INSTANTLY FEEL FIERCE

Splurge a Little *Instead of your usual plain coffee, next time you're at Starbucks order some ridiculously delicious drink that costs you five dollars. Sometimes the smallest things, like a little treat, can completely cheer you up and make you feel good.*

Splurge a Lot! *Get together with a friend and go out for the most amazing lunch, and don't worry about what it will cost you. Relish this time with your friend and make an event of it.*

Accessorize *If you're not feeling so fabulous, accessories always make a difference. Get together with a friend and trade a few pieces of jewelry for a fun outfit pick-me-up. Or treat yourself to an adorable new wallet—it will make you smile every time you take it out of your bag.*

Dress Up *You're pretty much guaranteed to feel confident when you have somewhere great to go and you look the part. Make the getting-ready process an event in and of itself: Turn on music, pour yourself some champagne, and really get into it. I like to play some Britney and Rihanna and do a little runway walk in front of the mirror! Or just dress up like a fierce diva for work. Instead of your usual look on a dreary, rainy day (pants, a sweater, rain boots), put together an outfit that makes you feel fabulous!*

Best for Last, Lady: *Wear Heels* *I'm so serious about this one. A really amazing high heel makes a huge difference in confidence for most women. It literally puts you on a pedestal. It's like having your own platform. You have to carry yourself in a certain way to even walk in high heels, so that instantly helps you to feel fierce. Even if you're not the type to wear heels all the time, just try it once. Practice at home if you're afraid of heights, then wear 'em outdoors and walk tall.*

The Miracle of Makeup!

Before *Project Runway* I worked at the Stila makeup counter in New York City, and I made a great discovery. Through working with hundreds of women every week, I learned that, more than your wardrobe or accessories, makeup is one of the best ways to feel fierce in a flash.

FEARLESS TIP:* *Makeup provides a great boost in feeling fierce because it can take you away from the real world. When you wear it, you can be anybody you want.

Why makeup? There's an instant gratification with cosmetics. Maybe one day you're rocking a fabulous crazy red lip, and the next day you have a sultry, smoky eye to go out on the town. How fun is that? And the best part about makeup is that you can take it off in a matter of seconds. Don't like that dark lip? It's gone. Not feeling fierce in the purple mascara you tried on a whim? Erase it. You can take makeup off so quickly that every day (or every hour, if you're experimenting) you can be a different character and find a great new way to feel fierce. I *love* that about makeup! How else can you play a different role by doing something as simple as changing your eye shadow or your lip color? So fabulous!

Beauty products can also make you feel fierce because they're something to indulge yourself in. Pampering yourself always feels good, and the way it makes you look (more important, how you *think* it makes you look) can directly affect the way you feel. So the next time you've had a rough, stressful week at work, skip the shopping that will empty your wallet and see if you can find something as small and inexpensive as an amazing lipstick that'll make you feel like a top model!

MAKEUP MUSTS!

1 Mascara is key. It changes your entire face and opens it up. I love Dior mascara. Stila has [illegible] good one, too, and Bobbi Brown'[illegible]cara is very natural.

2 A little color fo[illegible]e is really great. It can be [illegible]er or some color on the c[illegible]u can get fabulous powder, br[illegible] blush from anywhere—ev[illegible]et! And I love an all-ove[illegible]r from Victoria's Secret Bea[illegible]

3 Finally, a fabulo[illegible]s great on every woma[illegible] good lip gloss, and M•A•C [illegible] have an amazing range o[illegible]

Department Store Delights

If you've got the time and you want an extraspecial confidence booster, hit up your local department stores—they are the best part of life! Why not go on a little trip and hit every department store in your city? How fun would that be? Your destination: the makeup counters. It's a makeup artist's job to create a fantasy for you, and if they're good, they'll really want to. So sit back and be pampered! Play with the products and notice how easy it can be to feel fierce. But don't be cheap, lady—you've got to buy something. The tickity tack* women who sit at the counter and get a full face but don't buy anything? That's *not* cute!

All right, divas, we need a quick time-out from all the talk of makeup and high heels. We need to butch this book up a bit here. Even the manliest men deserve to feel fierce! So here are some key manly-man items and activities to help you guys to feel fierce (according to yours truly, anyway), and where to find 'em.

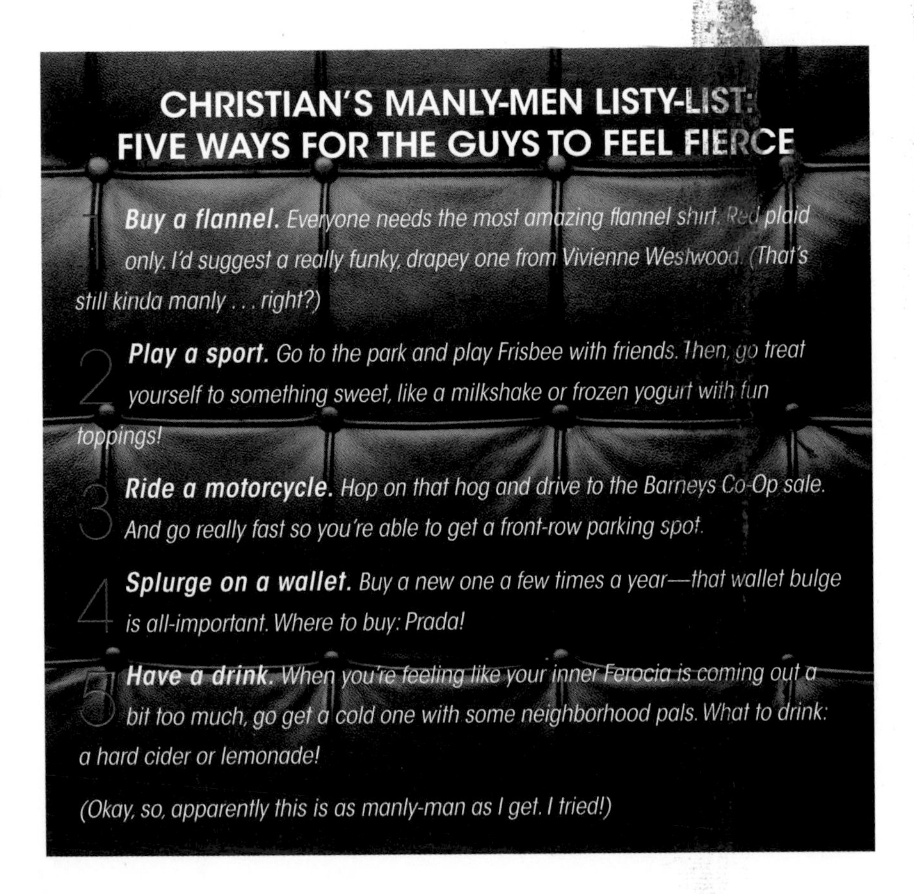

CHRISTIAN'S MANLY-MEN LISTY-LIST: FIVE WAYS FOR THE GUYS TO FEEL FIERCE

1. **Buy a flannel.** *Everyone needs the most amazing flannel shirt. Red plaid only. I'd suggest a really funky, drapey one from Vivienne Westwood. (That's still kinda manly . . . right?)*
2. **Play a sport.** *Go to the park and play Frisbee with friends. Then, go treat yourself to something sweet, like a milkshake or frozen yogurt with fun toppings!*
3. **Ride a motorcycle.** *Hop on that hog and drive to the Barneys Co-Op sale. And go really fast so you're able to get a front-row parking spot.*
4. **Splurge on a wallet.** *Buy a new one a few times a year—that wallet bulge is all-important. Where to buy: Prada!*
5. **Have a drink.** *When you're feeling like your inner Ferocia is coming out a bit too much, go get a cold one with some neighborhood pals. What to drink: a hard cider or lemonade!*

(Okay, so, apparently this is as manly-man as I get. I tried!)

9 CONCLUSION: THINKING BIG

Every once in a while, I don't feel fierce* at all, and there's no easy fix to turn it around. There are always times when you're not feeling confident or accomplished. It just depends on what's happening in your life. Personally, if I'm not making any clothes in a given week or I'm not doing a good job on a piece that I'm working on, it can be completely frustrating. But you have to think about it like this: There are so many hours in a day, so many days in a week, so many weeks in a month, and so many months in a year. I like to think about what's going to be, not necessarily what is at the moment. If I'm feeling really bad about something but it's not going to be the same situation in a month or a year, then I just make the decision not to feel that way. Why should I stress my day away about this one thing that's bumming me out?

Fearless (Celebrity!) Tip

"Surround yourself with positive people. Negativity breeds negativity. Focus on what you want and where you want to be, not what you *don't* want. This is a waste of time. You'd be surprised at how you will attract more confident people when you become confident yourself. I always tell people if you don't believe in yourself, how do you expect anyone else to believe in you?"

—KIMBERLEY LOCKE

I like to look at the big picture because I have big dreams. And because I have big dreams—like wanting to become a famous fashion designer who everyone wears—why would I listen to that person who makes fun of me for having spiky hair? Or why would I get depressed over a difficult week? I wouldn't, because I'm looking at a big picture. Sometimes you just have to ride out the funk, trannies,* and keep your eye on the prize. The fierce feeling will return! Trust.*

PART THREE

Every Day Is a Runway . . . Work It

Now that you're looking flawless* and feeling like a rock star, it's time to complete the fierce* trifecta and start truly walking the walk—*acting* fierce. Each part goes hand in hand, after all, so you have to truly feel fierce before you can act it. So go back to Part Two if you need, trannies.* Otherwise, read and rock on!

10 TAKE CHANCES

First and foremost, if you're going to act fierce* you have absolutely got to take chances. You can't be safe all the time. Remember: Fear and fierce are polar opposites. If you're afraid of taking chances you can't ever be fierce.

If You Have Nothing to Lose

This is the easiest time to take a chance in life. If you want to take a gamble on something and you have nothing to lose (say, trying out for a reality show—hello!—or taking a part-time or volunteer position in a new field), then there really is very little holding you back. The only thing that might keep you from doing that sort of thing is *you*. Everyone is scared of making mistakes and looking foolish, but you have to learn to cast those fears aside and just go for it—because if you have nothing to lose, you have everything to gain.

Fearless (Celebrity!) Tip

"The most important thing about how you present yourself to the world is the way you feel about yourself. Don't be phony, say what you mean, and above all be comfortable, because if you aren't comfortable that's when you get an attitude."

—WHOOPI GOLDBERG

Runway-Bound!

One of the biggest, most fabulous* ways that I took a chance was auditioning for *Project Runway*. So when the opportunity came about one day during lunch with my friends—and I had nothing to lose—I told myself, "Who cares how this turns out? I'm just going to go for it."

It was March 2007, and I was living in New York after graduating from college in London. And as much as I wanted to be well on my way to starting the House of Siriano, I was working at the SoHo Bloomingdale's in downtown Manhattan as a Stila makeup artist, taking things one day at a time and dreaming about what I'd rather be doing with my life.

FEARLESS TIP:* *If you have nothing to lose, tell yourself "Who cares?" and just go for it.

Then one day I was out to lunch at Lazzara's Pizza (the most amazing pizza in the world—definitely check it out when you're in New York!) with my friend Jersey, and "Park Avenue," my diva friend. She said to me, "The *Project Runway* auditions are in two days—you have to go!" I thought about it for about 2.5 seconds and replied, "Yeah, you're right. I should." It was as simple as that! I wrote down the address on the paper tablecloth, tore it off, and

headed home. *So* random, right? Then I filled out the forms online, and I called a friend from Bubbles to be my model at the audition.

Even though I had nothing to lose by trying out (since, really, what was the worst that could happen? I wouldn't make it and I'd go back to work at Stila?) those nagging questions still swirled through my head: What will the judges think of my work? What if they hate it? What if they hate *me*? But I kept telling myself "Who cares?" and picked out clothes for the audition that *I* liked: a super chic black wool and cashmere blazer, a futuristic-looking black-and-silver dress in a marbled fabric that I'd made that night (we ended up using that very same fabric in the *Project Runway* team challenge—for Team Star!), and a blouse that I made in London. To this day, I still use that pattern for the body of a blouse—Becki Newton wore it on *Ugly Betty*! (Even designers have their own signatures!)

As you can see, auditioning for *Project Runway* was totally random. But I took a chance and went into it without fear because even if I were laughed out of the judging room, I'd have a new experience under my belt. And a new dress, too!

As a result of my attitude going into the *Project Runway* audition, I felt so much more confident and comfortable because I knew I could always tell myself those two little words: "Who cares?" Maybe the judges would hate my work. But I truly wouldn't lose anything from the experience. Obviously everyone wants to succeed and be fabulous at everything they try, but that just isn't realistic. Sometimes you'll be flawless* and sometimes you'll be a hot mess.* But you have no chance at the flawlessness if you don't go for it. And that, lady,* is acting fierce.

If You *Do* Have Something to Lose

Sure, it's easier to take a chance when there are little to no repercussions. But when there are, you have to look at the situation carefully and ask yourself what you're getting out of it. It's just a matter of weighing the benefit against the risk. Look at designers: More often than not, they take risks in their work because they'll have a chance at greatness. Staying safe and inside the lines rarely results in fabulousness!

Celebs Chancing It

Very often when celebrities take chances in their careers, they can stand to lose a lot: money, prestige, fame. If you're the star of a bunch of huge blockbuster movies and then the next day you take a role in a weird, low-budget movie that nobody likes, that's a big risk. But I think it's one worth taking because you can look at what you've done before and still say, "Who cares?" You've done so much that you're allowed to take that risk. Look at Madonna—she's done a million amazing things with her career, and you can tell she doesn't care what people think of her anymore. (How fierce is *that*?) So the more you do, the easier it will be to say those two words, even when you do have something to lose.

Say them out loud if that helps you—remember, no paparazzi following you! Who. Cares.

Even if you're not Madonna, if you've got something to lose, it's just a matter of considering the big picture. For my second collection at New York Fashion Week, I wasn't going to throw caution to the wind and take a giant "Who cares?" risk, because as a new designer I can't risk a giant mistake. So I took chances *within* my collection, just not in the same way that I would in a nothing-to-lose situation. I had three crazy ruffled dresses in there—not thirteen. When I've had a few more collections behind me, I may take an edge-of-the-cliff risk and go for some big, crazy theme and tell myself (and the critics), "Who cares?" But for my second collection and my third—Egyptian-inspired—collection, I took risks where I could.

Fearless (Celebrity!) Tips

"I hear so many women say, 'This isn't something I would normally wear,' like that's a bad thing. If you wear it, it is therefore something you would wear! So the more you wear and do new things, the more you can get away with."

—BECKI NEWTON

"Being comfortable in whatever you're wearing is the key in presenting yourself to others. I have fun on the red carpet and embrace whatever character I'm channeling. Could be a chanteuse, an opera diva, a flapper, or a flower child. But once you decide, commit to it!"

—VANESSA WILLIAMS

11 FINDING YOUR PATH

Pave Your Own Runway

People don't hand you things all that often in life. So sometimes it's about finding that runway less traveled, or even creating your own. Everyone hits roadblocks—situations, places, and people that won't let you get what you want. But when there's a will . . . you know the rest of that saying, trannies.* Always consider whether you can make your own option if the right one doesn't exist. I've been doing it since high school.

Costume Couture

Even before I decided to go to design school for college, I was really interested in fashion. But Baltimore isn't exactly the mecca of the industry, so I found my own way to get to design—through Bubbles.

Every year in Washington, D.C., Bubbles competes in the local hair show, Hair Wars. A hair show is basically a competition among all the stylists and salons in the area to see how creative you are. And it's judged on many things beyond just hair: makeup, beauty, clothing, style, and music.

Now, even though Annapolis was one of the top salons in the

the hair show. *Cloud nine.* It was my first time doing a show like that, and the costumes turned out fine. They were almost entirely glued together, not sewn, but whatever! The show was fabulous,* but we didn't get that coveted win. Still, I had gotten a taste of designing and I was on my way. Armed with inexperienced determination (that's the best kind, isn't it?—that's when there's really no fear!), I set out to win it the following year.

By the time the next show rolled around, they let me do everything—the costumes and the makeup and the choreography and the look of the whole show. We made it really themed-out—African tribal. The fantasy hairstyles were these elaborate zebras and birds. It was like *The Lion King*! Fabulous! It was probably the best show ever (if I do say so myself!), perfectly choreographed, and the costumes were amazing. And, drumroll, please . . . we won first place.

I'd go on to coordinate the next two hair shows for Bubbles—right before I left for college in London and then during *Project Runway*. Let me tell you, trannies, I was on a roll. I did a shipwrecked pirates theme for one year, which was *so* fabulous. And get this—we won two more times! So even though I was designing costumes, not clothes, I got a taste of the world I so desperately wanted to be a part of. So once again, I said "Who cares?" and celebrated getting my start in fashion the only way I knew how.

Making the Grade

A similar situation came up my senior year in high school when the right option wasn't there for me and I had to make my own. At my high school, the Baltimore School for the Arts, you can do a directed study your senior year, which is like a major in college. Most of the students would do photography, painting, illustration, things like that. But I wanted to do fashion design for my directed study, which they did not offer.

They turned me down, of course, so I took matters into my own hands and figured out a way to make it work for me. I proposed to my teachers: Why don't I do fashion sketching in drawing class? And paint fashion figures in painting class? And for art history class (which I was so bad at—trust),* I convinced the head of the art department to let me write essays on fashion in the eighteenth century. So I basically made my own program! I even created an "internship" for myself, which consisted of working at the salon and helping with alterations and visuals at Banana Republic.

And then for my thesis project at the end of the year, I suggested to my teachers that I do a fashion show. Talk about an ideal final exam, right? So I showed a collection in an art gallery at the school. I had about ten models, and I had my salon girls from Bubbles do the hair and the makeup. And all the clothes were stretch jersey and other easy, easy fabrics to deal with because I still wasn't so good with the sewing at the time! That would later improve, of course, but the collection was still fabulous!

So the Christian Siriano program at the Baltimore School for the Arts (it's not really called that, but it should be—I love that!) was attended by me and me alone. Nobody else has done it since. An exclusive! How fabulous.

And check this out—it paid off for the school in the end. I did an auction there in 2008, and two women bid $25,000 each for an outfit I would create. I raised $50,000 for the school! What up now?! My tuition was like, $4,000 a year for three years, so they ended up making my total tuition times four! Givin' back!

Confronting Challenge

It's important to act fierce in both the good times and the bad. If you're only fabulous when things are going well, you're half-assing it, lady! Acting fierce also means confronting and overcoming challenge and disappointment.

Rejected!

After my junior year of high school, I packed up, said good-bye to my little nautical town in Maryland, and moved to New York City to attend the FIT summer program (that's Fashion Institute of Technology, in case you didn't know, trannies). It was during those three months that I came to truly fall in love with New York. (I even lived on the Lower East Side about two blocks away from the apartment you saw on *Project Runway*!) So I spent my summer taking classes, being challenged in fashion, and basically living my dream.

So as high school wrapped up, I naturally wanted to go back to FIT. I remember going to portfolio review during the application process and they really loved my work—they even talked about giving me a presidential scholar award. But then, the unthinkable happened. I. Didn't. Get. In. It was devastating. I was like, what is going on *here*? I suppose it was based on my grades, but I really

FEARLESS TIP:

Disappointment can lead to new opportunity. So if you don't get into your number one school, or you don't land that dream job you've been obsessing over, or even if you break up with that amazing person you thought you'd be with forever, remember that some of the best things in life are born from a downright bummer.

don't know. When you're not accepted to a school, a lot of times you never really know why. I was so mad at New York. I couldn't get back in to that city I'd come to love so much, and there were no other colleges or universities that appealed to me there.

The rejection was a heavy blow. And for a long time, I was pretty embarrassed about it, so I didn't tell anybody that I wasn't accepted. I'd just be like, "Oh yeah, I didn't want to go to FIT." At the time, I thought *that* was acting fierce—playing off my failures and acting like everything was my decision. But do you know what's even more fierce? Accepting your losses and looking forward to what may come next.

Just two days after the FIT rejection (College 1, Christian 0), I went online and searched fashion design schools in London. To this day, I don't know why I chose London. I don't have any sort of connection to the city, I'd never been there, and I didn't even know who London fashion designers were! After the New York fiasco I asked my teacher, "Where is a cool place to go for fashion design?" And she said, "Oh, you should go to Europe." But in most of Europe they speak a different language, so London was kind of the only option!

And so I found American Intercontinental University and I applied. I said, "Mommy, Daddy, I'm going to move to London.

FEARLESS TIP TO MOM: Don't worry—I'm working it out in New York City. It's totally fabulous. Love you!

What do you think?" My family was so shocked that they didn't know what to do. So they let me go. (It's funny because my mother worries about me more now that I'm in New York than when I lived in Europe. She calls me every day!)

The moral of the story? Sometimes taking chances means actually lucking into something after being rejected or facing a tough challenge. I wouldn't trade my experience in London for anything, and I had to go through a bitter disappointment to get there.

Get Competitive

My rejection from FIT made me really mad, and it made me want to work harder. I thought, "Oh, well, then screw *them*." And the big picture was that I wanted to go to fashion school (remember: I always look at the big picture). So if not New York, then fine: I'll go to school somewhere else! I'll go all the way to *London*. How do you like that?! I've always been that type of person: If something doesn't happen for me I become really, really determined to do something more fabulous to make that first option look totally stupid. And I think that's actually the best way to be. I'm competitive but not necessarily with others. I compete with myself to make myself better and my goals bigger and bigger. See if you can do the same, and try to best yourself whenever possible.

FEARLESS TIP:

See if you can best yourself. Sure, it can be motivational to compete with other people, but try beating your own best score. In the long run, it may help you even more than competing with others.

Be ***BOLD***

If you have the desire, forget about fitting into the norm or falling within the usual. Other than self-doubt and fear, really, what's holding you back from doing anything? For some reason, I'm just not afraid to do something on my own or do something different. To me, that's acting fierce. And really I think it should be like that with anybody, even if you're not a fashion designer or not into fashion at all—even if you're just looking for a new job or want a change in life. You *have* to be bold because that's how you get noticed. That's how new, exciting, and fabulous things happen.

***FEARLESS TIP:* Even if something seems out of your league or out of the ordinary, be bold and go for it.**

Setting the Stage

When I first started at American Intercontinental University, my days were all about learning the basics. You go to basic sewing classes, and basic drama classes, and I was a little ahead of the basics just from going to an art school for three years. So I was really bored. I wanted to do something fabulous and fun. The solution? I put together a little fashion show five months into my freshman year and staged it during London Fashion Week. It was low budget, and I showed in a club that I'd rented out for a night (my dad helped me out with the money—thanks, Dad!). It was tough and it wasn't cheap, but it was worth it.

The audience was mostly friends of mine, students and tutors, but it was cool and I felt like it was a big accomplishment. I launched a Web site from it, I had all these clothing samples to use in finding a job, and, most important, one of my teachers noticed the work I was doing. She had heard about my fashion show through other tutors and teachers who had told her that it had gone really well. This teacher had worked at Vivienne Westwood for ten years, and she told me she thought I'd be wonderful there. So my fashion show was key to me getting a job at Vivienne!

12 BRINGING THE FIERCENESS TO THE REAL WORLD

Hopefully you've found your path in life and you're forging your way to fierceness.* Now I hate to tell you this, but as you may know (or will soon find out) the real world is not all it's cracked up to be. There are lots of tough lessons to learn out there—I'm still learning them myself. But fear not: There are ways to maintain the fierceness out there.

Rocking It as the Newbie

Make Yourself Invaluable

Being an invaluable member of your workplace instantly ups your fierce factor. Simply put, if people can't live without you, they're going to think *really* highly of you. So get yourself acting fierce in a way that no one can ignore. If work is not the same without you, that's fabulous!*

Do It All

When I first started at Bubbles I worked as a shampoo tech. I would do assistant duties, apply toners and color and, of course, shampoo. Some days shampooing wasn't all that cute, but if you're working in a high-end salon like Bubbles it's not like you're doing five dollar haircuts and washing Elmer Fudd's hair. So I really got into it, and I came to be such a fast worker. I had so much energy every single day that I could shampoo about five clients at once! And I would make more money in my tips than the stylists would. The clients (and my bosses) *loved* it! And then when I became a receptionist, I was just as fast at that job. I could answer the phones really quickly, and whenever one of the clients was really mad and the stylists were being bitchy, they'd say, "Christian, you talk to them!" And I'd be like, "*Lady!** Love you, calm down." To me, being able to pull out anything you need to be invaluable—even making a silly joke to defuse a situation—is pretty fierce.

FEARLESS TIP:
At some point, you're gonna be the new guy or gal at a job. It's not easy and it's not glamorous, but it's one of those times in life that you've got to just grit your teeth, do it, and learn.

Get Organized, Lady!

Being organized is about more than just aesthetics or cleanliness. Keeping your home and your workplace very clean and organized is important because it helps keep your life sane. You can find things more quickly, be totally on top of your work, and make your days go a little more smoothly. One of the reasons I was so valued at Bubbles was because I was incredibly organized. More than anyone else in that salon, I knew when *every* appointment was scheduled, and it wouldn't have been that way had I not been so organized.

An Extra Five Minutes

Who doesn't need this in their life? I know I do—in fashion, an extra five minutes can be like a lifetime. Sometimes you need them to get to that meeting with Victoria Beckham! But regardless of what industry you're in, those five minutes can be key. If you waste them at your house looking for your keys, then maybe you won't make the light, and then you'll get held up in traffic and miss the important meeting that would have landed you your big promotion! Every minute really does count. So preserve them by keeping everything organized in your home and office. Put your keys in the same place every day, keep your work materials filed all together, the kids' school paperwork all in one spot . . . you get the idea. It shouldn't be stressful keeping track of those minutes. *Au contraire,* keeping track of them actually makes you feel like you have *more* time, since you'll be rushing around less, and who doesn't want that?

Learn the Ropes—But Pretend You Already Know Them

That way you can learn more than you would by asking questions. When you're working things out for yourself, you're figuring out *how* things work, which will serve you better in the long run. But it's not just about trying to look good or pretending to be someone you're not. I really think it's good for anyone learning a new skill, especially in the arts, to figure things out on their own when they can.

FEARLESS TIP: It's good to ask questions, but it's great to figure things out on your own.

Beading Fierce

My first internship in London was with this little design company called Ben Maher. Ben was a new designer at the time, and he did couture. It was my freshman year and I was on top of the world. I remember he was really tough on me. He would give me these extremely hard projects, and I was still learning the ropes so it was difficult. It was all couture and hand beading and really beautiful fabrics, so it was like total candy for me—but completely overwhelming, too. I remember doing fittings and the model castings, and I learned a lot from being in those situations.

But, as green as I was, I always pretended I knew what I was doing! And I'm really good at that. Even if I have no idea what I'm doing, I make it look like I'm a pro. For a while, all Ben would give me to do was hand beading. But I'd never done any hand beading in my life! So in a matter of weeks I went from never hand-beading a single piece to hand-beading an entire dress. I just figured it out. It's how I've always had to do it. Give it a try!

Learning the Hard Way

Sometimes there's just no way around this. It would be great if every lesson learned in the real world involved some fabulous personal triumph, but that's just not realistic, lady. Everyone has to learn the hard way. I did, and I did it while working for two of my most favorite designers.

VIVA VIVIENNE!

Next stop on my internship circuit? Vivienne Westwood. I loved Vivienne and was totally psyched to be there, but it seemed like every little thing there was a challenge. First off, most of my coworkers didn't speak English. A lot of Vivienne's pattern makers were German, so they spoke German to each other all day long! The language barrier was particularly difficult because I didn't know very much at all about the business when I started there, so chatting with them would have been helpful.

But I would still come to learn a *lot* at Vivienne. We had to copy patterns and cut out pieces all the time. It was a lot of tedious work, and I didn't really know what I was doing, but I picked it up along the way. Plus, there were *so* many interns that you always had the feeling that you needed to do better than the next person, and some of them had been there for like six months when I had been there for a day.

There were definitely moments that I asked myself, "What am I doing?" Being new at any job or internship isn't easy, because the people you work with will say things like "Go photocopy this." Period. No more information. And you don't have any idea where the copy machine is! So that part of it wasn't too much fun. But beyond the frustration, every day that I went to work I learned something new. Even if it was just where to find the sewing machine or how to cut a pattern, I knew I'd be using this stuff down the line, so I worked hard at it.

McQueen Dreams

After Vivienne Westwood, I took an internship with Alexander McQueen. Fabulous! He is my favorite designer to this day, by far. But when I started out at McQueen I had a very tough boss. (Most everyone is tough in the fashion world—you get used to it!) So Ms. Tough Boss told me, "We're going to do a three-day trial with you to see if you can hack it." I told you people in fashion are a different breed! But I am, too—and I always love to prove myself—so McQueen had met his match in me!

Until my first assignment, that is. They gave me a sample blouse to work on that would be pinned up on a board for inspiration. It was a crazy white ruffled blouse, silk crepe, and it had fifty pin tucks on each side. The blouse had piping, and the buttons had to be perfectly dyed to match, and it had to be ruffled. Meanwhile, just like the hand beading at Ben Maher, I had never even sewn a pin tuck before. It was a little scary, but I figured out the hand beading, so how hard could this be?

Turns out, extremely hard. So I would ask very basic questions, but I didn't exactly get a support group to help me. And they wanted it completed that day, in between all the other assignments they were giving me! It was: Run here, go there, pick this

up . . . so I had to keep putting the blouse down. I'd get back from an errand and the sewing machine would be taken. My deadline was looking further and further out of reach.

The blouse took me three days to finish. I was *so* upset about how hard it was and that I couldn't complete it at lightning speed that I cried in the bathroom. I'm talking crying every day for the first few days. But when I wasn't camped out in the loo, I was working as hard as I could, and finding out that making clothes is not as easy as whipping out my trusty glue gun to put together costumes for Hair Wars. Not being able to meet the deadline was superannoying and really scary. But people didn't know about my mini-breakdowns—I played that off really well. Even so, times were tough. I still didn't know what I was doing (welcome to your first few jobs) and I was like, "Why am I here? I hate fashion. I want to die." (Real world 1, Christian 0.)

But *then*, in between the crying jags and the near meltdowns, I finished the blouse. And it was fabulous! They pinned it up on the board like they'd planned and it was one of the samples that they re-created for the show that season! It really looked great—I could not have been more pleased.

JUKI

Where's the "Fabulous"?

In the real world, you won't always get praise for a job well done. It's sad but true, I know. Coming right out of school, most young professionals thrive on positive reinforcement, so it can be a nasty shock to find that you don't always get that at work. Welcome to the real world. We're not in the spoon-fed, feel-good land of University anymore, Toto!

So here I am at McQueen, victorious after finishing the sample blouse. As it turned out, Ms. Tough Boss didn't really care that it took me three days to complete it—they just made it seem like they really needed it ASAP. I guess that was part of my three-day trial to see if I could hack it. So I triumphantly turned in my assignment and waited with contented anticipation for the praise I so deserved. Five minutes later, my boss inspected my impeccable work and said, "Oh, great. Now, can you sew these other things?"

Wait, wait, wait. *What?!* I was stunned. That was it? How about "It's fabulous, Christian"? Or "Wow, it's wonderful"? Or even just a simple "Thank you"? Nothing, nada, zilch. *Great.* My praise for all the hard work, all the crying, and my eventual victory was

"Now, can you do *this*?" I was ready to cry all over again. I moved on to the next project, still reeling from my lack of accolades. I had *soooo* wanted a "Fabulous job!" I didn't get it. My response, of course, was typical: Screw this. *What-ever.*

And from that point on, whenever I had an assignment, I would do it really fast so that my bosses would say, "Oh, well, okay, I have to give him something else." And they didn't always have something else to give me! I didn't get that praise I so desired, but I think I proved myself to them anyway, and it felt really good. In fact, that was actually how it became my thing to be really fast at doing projects, like I did on *Project Runway*!

Be Ready to Network

You never know what people do outside of work or who they know, so always keep your eyes and ears open and a smile on your face. And in pursuit of any dream you may have, you need to be prepared to take that job or internship that isn't exactly what you want to do, so keep in mind that there may be more than meets the eye.

FEARLESS TIP:
Opportunity breeds opportunity. Almost any job has the potential to lead to something more.

New Opportunities

I wanted nothing more than to be working for a designer right out of school, but it didn't happen. Instead, I got the job doing makeup for Stila. The job paid well, but it meant dealing with cheesy tourists all day. I mean, really, how many people need a smoky eye palette? That's boring. (And you know how I feel about boring, lady!) So that's what I would do all day long, a shimmery eyebrow and a shimmery cheek and a shimmery lip and a glossy pink craziness. I craved more variety, I'll tell you that! But I was doing it to pay the bills, and that was fine. Still, there was something even better around the corner.

Thanks in part to Stila, I got into making wedding gowns. One day, a couple months into my Stila stint, one of the managers who worked at the counter told me she was getting married, and we started chatting about her wedding during work. I asked what her dress looked like, and she told me, "I got it for sixty dollars on sale at a bridal store, but I kind of want to do something to it, which is why I bought it so cheap." So, of course, I offered to do it for her. We decided to add pleating in the back and a train. And then I did this big veil for her—we even went shopping together to buy the fabric, and it was superfun!

Then from that I decided, oh, I like bride! Bridal gowns are fun! I ended up making several more for friends, and a new opportunity was born. It came from networking and keeping my eye out for new opportunities.

Work It Socially

The first part of your first impression is your entrance. So for your convenience, here are some tips for your grand arrival.

***FEARLESS TIP:* Whether you're going to a party, to work, or even to school, first impressions are everything when it comes to acting fierce.**

Fearless (Celebrity!) Tips

"How to make a grand entrance? Pretend you've already been wherever you have to show up. (Even if it's the first time.) Hold your head up high and look at people in the room like you know them and you belong there. Then grab a cocktail and enjoy the looks that people throw your way. Be subtle, alluring, and mysterious."

—VANESSA WILLIAMS

"Plant two feet on the floor, walk forward, and don't fall."

—WHOOPI GOLDBERG

"Always smile and have good posture."

—NIKI TAYLOR

"I learned early on that no matter how amazing your outfit, hair, and makeup are, all of it can be ruined by bad posture. I used to round my shoulders and hunch over when I got nervous, and it looked awful. But one day, while wearing a so-so outfit, I remembered to throw my shoulders back and keep my head up, and my outfit looked like the most fabulous creation of all time. It really is *how* you wear clothes more than what you wear."

—BECKI NEWTON

Talk to People You Don't Know

For both social and networking purposes, I think that engaging with everybody at an event and learning little bits about people is a really good idea. And even if you don't remember their name during an entire dinner party, you'll learn something about them. I think it's often more important to remember a tidbit about a person than their name. Sounds a little crazy, I know, but you can't fake a genuine interest in what someone has to say, and coming by that honestly is so important. (You can, however, fake knowing his or her name—you can always ask someone else to remind you of what it is!)

Fearless (Celebrity!) Tips

"Always be nice and remember all your manners."

—NIKI TAYLOR

"Acting fierce is a matter of engagement. No matter what we're doing, we're interacting. It's important to demonstrate a full engagement with either an individual or a group of people. That means good eye contact, it means listening skills, it means respect for the other parties, and it means sincere, profound engagement (as opposed to just being a solo act with other people around you). If you do all of that, people will respond to you positively. You'll command the room. You'll own it without dominating it and without sucking all the air out of the room, in a manner of speaking!"

—TIM GUNN

Knowing When to Say No

Sometimes, of course, there can be nothing fabulous in what you're doing in the real world. But getting out of a bad situation isn't easy. It can be really hard to say no to things. The idea of not completing a job or an assignment is scary. We're taught in school that you should never say no and that you should please your bosses and always try your hardest, no matter what the circumstance. But sometimes, knowing when to say no can be your best asset. Imagine that you are a celebrity with agents, managers, and publicists working for you. When opportunities come up, the first thing they would ask on your behalf is what *you* would be getting out of the experience. Asking yourself that question and putting yourself first, with or without a management team behind you, is the first step toward figuring out when to say no to something

Photocopy Purgatory

Right after we were done shooting *Project Runway* and I knew I was one of the finalists, there were several months of downtime. I'd be designing my collection for the show, but I needed to do something else as well (gotta get paid!). So I took an internship with Marc Jacobs. I was happily willing to go down the intern road again because it was Marc—he's hugely successful. I knew I'd surely learn something.

I set out on my first day at Marc Jacobs, excited about designing my collection for *Runway* but still humble: I was only twenty-one, after all, and I couldn't wait to see what I could learn from this new position.

Day one: I am presented with ten humongous boxes of fabric samples, and my boss says, "We need to document these samples, so go photocopy them. All of them." There were, and I'm not exaggerating, thousands of fabric samples. Thousands! And they wanted me to photocopy each one and put them in binders so we'd have documentation of all the fabrics. Still, I thought, "Fine, every early job involves photocopying and coffee fetching. No problem." I put my head down and got to work. Nine hours later, my first day was over and I had done nothing but photocopy.

Day two and on: Repeat day one.

I was at Marc Jacobs for one week. I hadn't seen anything but a photocopy machine. But in the meantime, I was working on my own collection for *Project Runway*. I knew I was overqualified for the position and would be more challenged somewhere else. My instincts were telling me that I needed a different job, and I had to trust myself to say no, leave the job, and move on to the next opportunity. So I did.

13 CONCLUSION: TURNING IT OFF

If you're the type of person who has to be on your game all week long at work, entertaining, or doing whatever you do, it's important to take some downtime and really, truly, embrace it. It's extremely hard to act fierce* when you're completely exhausted.

In a fabulous* life, you can often feel like you *have* to go out all the time. The truth is, you don't always have to do the most glamorous thing in order to act fierce. In fact, doing something totally unglam can be the best idea. Sometimes you just need time for yourself, especially if you're always "on" like I am. (Think about it like this: The downtime allows you to recharge the fierceness!)

I personally experienced this need to turn it off at an unusual time—right after winning *Project Runway*. The other finalists and I were still sequestered in a hotel for confidentiality reasons, so we couldn't go home. I had literally just gotten everything I wanted by winning and showing in the tents at Bryant Park at twenty-two years old. I was so excited I could hardly stand it. And then, oddly, when it was time to go to the wrap party, I went up to the hotel room instead. I was just so tired that I couldn't even think. I went up to the room and looked through the *Elle* magazine that everyone at the fashion show received in their gift bag on their seat. It was really funny! When you have to be on for twenty-four hours a day, sometimes you just need to turn it off. So in between the pages of *Elle*, I ate almost an entire box of my favorite snack—Yodels! Totally *not* glamorous, but it was just what I needed. So be kind to yourself and take a break when you can. It will make you that much more fierce.

FEARLESS TIP:
You don't always have to be superoutgoing or go out on the town all the time to act fierce.

OMENSWEAR
Nontransferable

PART FOUR

Inspire Me!!!!

Well, my divas, by now you should be looking, feeling, and acting totally fierce.* But before you unleash all that fabulousness* out in the world, I want to share with you some fearless final reasons that I've become the person I am today—my inspirations.

Inspirations are so important when it comes to being fierce. In determining the way that you look, feel, and act, you always need to be inspired. Inspirations are like your material for being a fierce diva! I'm sure you'll be able to see how my inspirations influenced my style, personality, and designs, and I hope that it will get you thinking about what inspires *you*.

Pop Culture Inspirations

Whether or not you're a budding designer—or even an artistic type—you can benefit from being inspired. Maybe a costume in a movie will inspire some new and unexpected wardrobe choices, or a character's actions on a TV show could motivate you to try something new in life, like a sport or hobby that you've never tried. Inspiration is everywhere and can manifest itself in so many ways.

Fearless (Celebrity!) Tip

"When people would say to me, 'I don't know where to find inspiration,' I'd tell them, 'Just open your eyes and wake up! It's there!' It can be the inside of an elevator or a tiled floor. In my years of teaching, I would say to my students, 'Movies! Books! Web sites! If it's summertime, just sit outside and have an iced tea or an iced coffee and watch people go by.' I mean, really, there should be inspiration everywhere."

—TIM GUNN

Movies and the Stage

As you know, one of the first times I was ever truly inspired was when I was just a kid, watching *The Wizard of Oz*. And I was completely enchanted by one costume in particular—Glinda's huge ball gown, of course! As the years went on, it became apparent that it was really costumes in general that inspired me. Whether it was Dorothy's ruby slippers or all of the ornate, detailed pieces in *The Nutcracker*, there's something about the whimsy of a costume that inspires my dramatic side and captures my imagination. It makes me want to create clothes and embrace that drama and attention to detail.

FEARLESS TIP:
Everywhere you look in pop culture, there are things that inspire. So don't just absentmindedly watch movies and listen to music and experience the arts—let them sink in and affect you in some way.

Let's Dance

I found another childhood inspiration, ballet, while my sister was at an audition one year at the Maryland Ballet Theater. I was running around downstairs while my sister danced, and I was wearing little shorts, a T-shirt, and some Converse shoes that day. I looked nothing like the boys auditioning for the ballet. But then a woman said to me, "Christian, put a number on and go upstairs." So I did, and I landed a part in *The Nutcracker* (over other boys who were actually ballet dancers, no less)! As it turned out, dance came very naturally to me, and I'm sure it helped that I'd always watched and admired my dancer sister! For the next four years, I danced in *The Nutcracker*. For three of those years, I played one of the children who come out onstage inside that big, fabulous dress. (Hmm, coincidence that I love crazy volume in dresses today?) I was in the costume room every single day—I loved the fantasy, the styles, and the fashion, so dance has always been a major inspiration.

TV, Trannies!

By high school, I'd outgrown the Munchkins, flying monkeys, and witches of *Oz*. Luckily, there to take their place were Carrie, Miranda, Charlotte, and Samantha of *Sex and the City*! There's lots to be inspired by on television, but when it comes to fashion, the ladies of *Sex* were it for me. Carrie Bradshaw was the *ultimate* fashion experiment. There were no boundaries in her closet—she wore everything and anything! Right from the start, I was in love. Carrie could wear a tutu, a maribou boa, and a snakeskin minidress all in one season! Fabulous!

Of course, the woman who brought all that fierce fashion to the screen was costume designer Patricia Field. Her "no boundaries" vision inspired me to be fearless as well. Because she takes risks whenever she wants: Patricia Field can even put a giant bird on a character's head and it's cool!

Not only was watching *Sex and the City* like browsing through the latest issue of *Vogue*, but it was also personally inspiring for me as a teenager. Isn't it great that in such a close-minded world that we live in, people *loved* that show? I think that's amazing because there are so many people who judge others all day long, but *Sex and the City* had these characters who dressed crazy and put their sex lives on display like Manolos in a store window. And everyone loved them anyway! As a free-spirited, crazy teenager myself, I remember thinking, "If this show is based on real women in New York City, then maybe I'll get to dress them one day!" I knew they were out there and that inspired me.

MEMORABLE TV MOMENTS

Television is the perfect match for fashion when it comes to memorable, inspiring moments. Here are a few of my favorite TV moments that have influenced fashion:

1. *Remember that Versace dress cut down to forever that Jennifer Lopez wore to the Grammys? Fierce!* * *(And a bit tranny* * *. . .)*

2. *And how about Bjork's swan dress at the Oscars? Most people thought it was a hot tranny mess,* * *but it represented dissenting views in fashion. Love that.*

3. *I'll always remember Britney's sequined see-through outfit that she wore at the MTV Video Music Awards in 2000. When she ripped off the suit and it looked like she was naked underneath—talk about drama and shock value!*

4. *The dramatic red dress with the crazy collar that Heidi Klum wore to the Oscars in 2008 is something that people will remember for a long time. It was like watching some kind of fashion transformation—supermodel to red-carpet Oscar diva! And of course, there was Heidi's moment in my dress at the Emmys (more on this later, divas). So fabulous.* *

Designers

Obviously, designers inspire me because I'm a fashion designer. But designers can inspire anyone in any way: Maybe this season's Proenza Schouler collection will inspire a change in your wardrobe, or maybe it will just inspire you to do something amazing in your own field. If you've never been to a fashion show in the tents at New York Fashion Week, I highly recommend you check it out. The lights come up, the music pumps through the space, and you're taken on a journey that the designer has created for you. Just seeing someone's work come to life like that can inspire you to be great at whatever you do.

The specific designers who inspire me each bring something different to fashion. It's not just the cut of a dress or the drape of a fabric. For me, it's about *their* inspirations, the woman they dress, and how they take the journey from an idea sketched on paper to a completed look walking down the runway.

Alexander McQueen

McQueen's clothes are the pinnacle of high fashion but never go over the top. His beaded pieces, silk underskirts, and sassy little cocktail dresses are so high-end and perfectly made.

Proenza Schouler

The Proenza designers, Jack McCollough and Lazaro Hernandez, are the epitome of young and hip, and it's the super chic girl they design for who really inspires me. The girl who wears Proenza is young, but she's so sophisticated and chic that people aren't really sure about her age. She's not a kid, but she's fresh and fashion-forward. Whoever their muse is, even if she's one hundred percent fictional, she inspires me and makes me excited about fashion and how it can transform people.

Rodarte

The Rodarte designers, Kate and Laura Mulleavy, do fashion as a total art form. One of the ways they create their clothes is by playing around with fabrics, and the end result can look like a painting or sculpture. Instead of designs for the mainstream, their clothes are organic, and they truly take risks. The fact that they stay true to their artistic sensibility inspires me to stay true to myself, too.

Yves Saint Laurent

When I think of Yves Saint Laurent I think of perfect clothing. It's made perfectly and it fits perfectly. The look may not be as organic or artistic as some designers', but it's as close to flawless* as clothes can be. And you know I love flawless!

Giles Deacon

Giles mixes wearability and avant-garde. Some of his looks can be so out there that you don't really know where his inspiration came from at all—and that sense of risk appeals to me. And then, out of the blue, there's a cute, wearable shift dress. The fact that he can dabble in both areas is incredible.

Vivienne Westwood

Vivienne is one of the few designers whose clothes and design aesthetic have remained the same from the start, but it never gets old. She's a designer who makes a solid staple even better every season—you see the same silhouette for years, but it gets better each time. I totally aspire to be like that someday. And she still stays true to her punk notions (she worked with the Sex Pistols, after all) but she does it without being cheesy. Not easy, trannies!

Art

Art is always one of the most inspirational mediums. In fact, my Spring 2009 collection was inspired, in part, by a painting. I can't even tell you what it was that drew me to the piece, but something about the colors spoke to me, and I used them in most of the collection. And from there, I was inspired by clouds and the sky—all the colors there found their way into my work. So it was really a combination of art and nature that influenced my collection.

Personally, I love Dali. I love to look at abstract paintings with lots of brushstrokes, because those paintings can be anything. You might see an intriguing shape in there, or you can simply say, "I like this color," and then you can incorporate it into your clothes and, really, your life. Maybe a color will be so attractive to you that you'll want to use it to paint your bedroom. So if you're at a museum or even just flipping through magazines, open your mind to the art you see—abstract, realistic, whatever it may be. You never know when something will jump out and inspire you.

And if you need some ideas about what museums to check out, my favorites include the British Museum in London and the Louvre in Paris. (I mean, everyone should go and see the *Mona Lisa.* Hello!) In New York I love the Met; the Temple of Dendur is so inspiring. And every time they have their costume exhibits you're sure to get inspired—I loved the *AngloMania* exhibit about British fashion. The *WILD: Fashion Untamed* exhibit was totally amazing, and the *Superheroes* exhibit practically made me want to design superhero costumes!

Music

Personally, music inspires me in creating a fashion show, and I think that it inspires people to be fabulous. There are just certain songs and beats that make you feel like you want to walk down a runway! (Oh, please, like you haven't done a runway walk through your bedroom. We all have, lady!)* I listen to a lot of music when I'm working, and sometimes I'll be like, "Ooh, that's

really fabulous," and I'll picture a model coming down the run-
way and it helps me see, mentally, what she's wearing and how it should look. Music can inspire you in any number of ways, but generally speaking, I think that music inspires moods. If you've had a really bad day at work, pop in your favorite upbeat CD and watch how it inspires you.

MY DESIGNING PLAYLIST

"Unusual You," Britney Spears
"Shattered Glass," Britney Spears
"Womanizer," Britney Spears (Brad Walsh remix!)
"Break the Ice," Britney Spears
"Radar," Britney Spears
"Piece of Me," Britney Spears
"Ooh Ooh Baby," Britney Spears
"Oh Mother," Christina Aguilera
"Dynamite," Christina Aguilera
"Single Ladies (Put a Ring on It)," Beyoncé
"Sweet Dreams," Beyoncé
"Available," Brad Walsh
"Do It in the Streets," Brad Walsh
"Control Me," Brad Walsh
"Just Dance," Lady GaGa
"Poker Face," Lady GaGa
"The Fame," Lady GaGa
"Wish We Were Older," Metro Station
"Disturbia," Rihanna
"Rehab," Rihanna
"Umbrella," Rihanna
"Let Your Head Go," Victoria Beckham

Personal Inspirations

Inspiration is more than just what you see on-screen and on the runways. Your own personal life experiences truly inspire and influence who you are.

London Calling!

My years in London provided me with major inspiration—I'm sure you can still see it in my style and designs today. London has a diverse continental feel: Italian women walking around the streets in the most pointy-toed stiletto heels you've ever seen and fierce little Prada glasses; platinum blonde Swedish women in hobo-style pieces and gladiator sandals shopping at Selfridges; fierce Asian women in their perfectly put-together looks—all those different cultures and styles thrown together were amazing to me. I think you're exposed to more culture and style just walking around London than anywhere else!

FEARLESS TIP:* *You can always look to your own life to be inspired.

There's also a sense of style freedom in London. The blogger and paparazzi presence there is nothing like the insanity of Los Angeles or New York City. What's liberating across the pond

is that nobody really cares about what you're wearing and what you're doing. Anna Piaggi and Hillary Alexander are some of the most eccentric women ever, and they're London divas. That's so inspiring. (Anna Piaggi, oh my God, is fabulous—if you don't know who she is, Google her to see what I'm talking about!)

Famous Clients

I'm lucky to have dressed numerous celebrities so early in my career, and each one has taught me something and inspired the pieces I made for them. Here's a selection of some of my fabulous, inspirational divas.

Heidi Klum: Turning It Down

Right off the bat, Heidi inspired me because she's so sexy and so chic but she's never trashy. She's the ultimate definition of the *supermodel.* But when I was designing for her, I wanted the look to be me, too. I wanted my work to be a little bit of Heidi Klum and a little bit of Christian Siriano. So I made her a bunch of things, and then the next day she tells me, "Oh, Christian, some of these pieces are too crazy. They can't *all* be *this* dramatic!" So I basically had to tone it down a bit. I made her tiny little minidresses and skintight trousers, and they turned out great. And I loved it because Heidi is probably the one person who can change my design aesthetic sometimes—and for the better.

I also learned to work fast with Heidi. Right after my Spring 2009 show, I did a fitting with her for the Emmys! She loved the gray chartreuse gown from the show, and she literally tried it on and that was it. It fit her perfectly, so we changed the zipper and called it a day! She wore it to close the Emmys, fresh off the runway, and it looked absolutely stunning on her.

Victoria Beckham: Aiming to Stand Out

When I worked with Victoria she truly inspired me in every which way. I would have given her my entire collection if she wanted it! I made a lot of clothes for her, but the items that really stand out in my mind were the ones *especially* for Victoria, like an extravagant, backless, black skinny ruffled dress. I just felt like it was dramatic and interesting and avant-garde and super chic. And even if she never wears it in her entire life, at least I know it's in her closet. I think for her I was inspired to create something different that she didn't already have. Because, really, Victoria Beckham has an endless closet, and she quite possibly may have a piece of clothing from every single designer in the entire world. It's hard to compete with that—but I was inspired to try.

Whoopi Goldberg: Changing It Up

Oh my gosh, dressing Whoopi to host the Tonys in 2008 was probably one of the biggest challenges of my design career because I had to please Ms. Whoopi Goldberg, a woman famous for her blousy jeans and big muumuu tops! But she said that for the Tonys, "I want to convey drama and I want to be fabulous." So we made her dramatic and fabulous! And underneath Whoopi's more shy, demure look, she is super chic and has the most fabulous legs in the world! And, even better, she showed them off, which I love. It was just so inspiring to see her branch out from her everyday style, and I loved the challenge of making her dramatic but classy and chic. And in case you missed it, Whoopi and those legs of hers *worked it out*!

Becki Newton: Hard vs. Soft

When I guest-starred on and designed for an episode of *Ugly Betty*, Becki wanted to wear a really fabulous, very signature Christian. So I made her outfit a definite signature look, but in terms of tweaking it for her it was a toss-up between making an outfit to fit her real-life personality, which is super, super sweet, or one that would fit the bad girl she plays on television. I love Becki as a TV bad girl, so I went in that direction. The outfit was hard, and really dark and dramatic, and it was similar to what was in my Fall 2008 collection for *Project Runway*, but I wanted it to be a little different for her. I made only small changes, but they worked for the character and for Becki herself. Those teeny form-fitting skinny pants and that pouffy-sleeved blouse totally worked for her, since she's totally hot! That was certainly another inspiration with Becki. Why not show off a fabulous body? Everybody needs to know about it!

Pink and the Pussycat Dolls: Dressing for Rock Stars!

With both of these clients, I had to take a lot of direction from their personas—they're rock stars, so that needs to be top of mind for me when I'm designing. They have an image that's key to who they are as artists. So for Pink, I made a performance coat for her appearance at the MTV Video Music Awards in 2008. She and her stylist wanted it to be really fabulous and dramatic, and they had a lot of ideas, so it was a real collaborative effort. The result was a beautiful, electric blue coat that was a real showpiece. I didn't personally get to fit her—there was a lot of back-and-forth with her stylist, which often happens with celebrities—but the result was beautiful.

And for the Pussycat Dolls, whom I dressed for the American Music Awards in 2008, I did get to do fittings, but their stylist had a lot of input, so again, it was all about collaborating. But it was a great partnership because the girls wanted to move away from

their usual style of dressing and be more high fashion. And since my clothes are romantic and feminine but also really strong—just like the girls—it was a great fit. The girls wore pieces from my Spring 2009 collection, and for Nicole (the head Pussycat Doll!) I made a strapless bustier gray dress with lots of volume and a touch of purple. Fabulous!

Vanessa Williams: Dressing the Character

With Vanessa Williams, who wore one of my dresses in the spring 2008 season finale of *Ugly Betty*, I was completely inspired by her character on the show. Vanessa's character, Wilhelmina, is every aspiring fashion designer's idea of the diva editor at a magazine.

So it was incredibly fun to dress her. I made her a power suit, but in a dress form. I wanted it to be super chic, fitted, sexy, and very feminine. She's a really powerful presence (both on and off the show!) so I wanted the outfit to be just as powerful as Vanessa and Wilhelmina. And since she's so gorgeous I was inspired by colors to complement her amazing skin, so I went with a creamy gold champagne color. Flawless!

Kimberley Locke: Dressing Quietly

When I worked with Kimberley, she was going to appear on *American Idol* to sing a fabulous ballad, and I knew it was time for a fierce gown. The look needed to be more haute couture and less cheesy prom (since reality TV can lean toward the cheese factor, and I wanted to up the ante for Kimberley). I think that dressing her was a bit of a challenge because she is more of an average American girl and not a teeny-tiny supermodel—that's the girl who designers learn to dress. But I absolutely loved it. And in meeting her and planning what I'd design, I thought about how she was going to belt out a ballad with her amazing, powerful voice so the dress, really, was more of a background for her. Sometimes dresses should stand out, but this one needed to be a little softer, a little quieter, but with a signature Christian edge.

Leigh Lezark: Sometimes It's Simple

I dressed Leigh, a DJ and New York nightlife diva, for my Spring 2009 show at Fashion Week. I made her a shirt that was silk-knit jersey, black, really slinky with a box-pleated shoulder that gave it a little drama, and she wore it with a fabulous high-waisted short. Totally simple, but sometimes that's all you need for a client. And Leigh loved it—so much so that she wore it not only to my show, but to others, like Zac Posen's!

Everyday Women

There are tons of real (i.e., not famous—yet!) women in my life who've inspired me. I always thought some of the clients that came into the salon were fabulous! Especially the older clients, because they were these totally chic, sophisticated women who always knew what they wanted.

Some of my teachers in London provided inspiration for me, too. I had one teacher, Christiane, who'd worked with Vivienne forever; she always wore leather pants, cowboy boots, and a drapey, weird Vivienne Westwood top. Every. Single. Day. The same outfit! Can you imagine? She also wore these big, weird glasses that were super-futuristic-looking (very Balenciaga) and totally clear—they almost looked like goggles but they were her glasses! She had a platinum bob and she was very German. And then, every now and again, she'd mix up her look and wear a Diane von Furstenberg wrap dress and stilettos. I remember thinking, "What is going through her head?" But I did love both her loyalty to her look and her ability to transform from time to time. It tied into my idea of fashion as fantasy, and just looking at her in class got my mind going about fashion and design.

And then there was Prudence, my fabulous millinery teacher (that means hat-making, divas) in London. She inspired my sense of craziness, my love of hats, and a desire for impeccability in my work. She'd look around our classroom going, "Oh my God, lovely, oh my God, lovely, lovely, lovely, lovely. Really, but everything is quite shit." All day long! She'd be like, "Christian, why'd you do that? It really is quite shit." Talk about an induction into the ruthless world of fashion, right? I think

she inspired me personally as much as she did fashion-wise. I loved her crazy, say anything attitude. Another slightly loony quality that I have to admit I totally admired was the way she maintained her accessories. She was just so perfect in that regard. She'd wear Prada every day, usually flat Prada shoes, and carry Yves Saint Laurent bags. And every night she would take her bag home, take everything out, put the tissue paper the bag came with back inside and put the bag in its box. That is someone who really appreciates fashion. I so admire that. And almost every day she'd be in her Prada trench coat and look totally put together. And if you said something about how much you liked it, she'd go, "Oh, no, this little thing? Oh, blast, it's Prada." She was beyond fabulous. Love her!

Hair Products

I figured I have to include this because everyone's always talking about my hair! The long and short of it is that I *love* products. No, I'm not literally inspired by hair spray, but like any kind of artist, I think you bring your creativity to all aspects of your life. And for me, it's my hair! There are just so many fun products out there and I want so many of them! And even though I only use about two products now (I've got the fashion hawk down to a *science*) I still love the sheer wealth of products that are out there to use!

So if you love products the way I do, let them inspire you to change up your look from time to time. They're these superfun tools that can change a boring hairdo into something fabulous. Try it out! There's nothing wrong with being inspired by hair, trannies. Look where it got me!

FABULOUS

15 FROM INSPIRATION TO GARMENT

This final chapter is geared more toward you fabulous* designers-to-be, and those divas out there who are interested in the design process. Think of fashion design as inspiration come to life!

The Road to the Clothes

Obviously, the inspiration-to-design process depends on the designer. Personally, I can look at a photograph of something really quickly, totally be inspired with an idea, and run with it. I don't even need to keep the photo as a reference. Of course, other times I'm looking at a *million* things and the inspiration just isn't there. We're only human, after all!

FEARLESS TIP: The pattern in which inspiration strikes is extremely random—that's why it's so difficult. It's a natural process, and things just happen when they happen.

As I was working on my Spring 2009 collection, for example, I was inspired by colors. I saw this weird painting in a design magazine, and I loved the blues and grays in it. The sky, too. Simple as that sounds, it was the colors and the textures of the clouds that got my imagination going. And then from the colors I thought, oh, it'd be really cool to layer them on top of each other, and it all sort of snowballed from there. I don't even have the picture of the painting anymore. I just saw it and I remembered it. And that's always been my thing. I have a little bit of a photographic memory—once I see something I'll always have it in mind.

Making Memories

And it came in especially handy during the avant-garde challenge on *Runway*, in which Chris March and I created the cream-colored dress made up of fabric circles and the huge, oversized neck piece/sculpture! I had never made a dress like that in my life. I had never even cut circles out of fabric before, but I just started cutting the circles, imagined what it might look like, and let 'er rip! And, somehow, it worked.

The same kind of thing happened with the hombre flounce ruffled dress in my Fall 2008 collection. I sewed one ruffle on a piece of fabric, and I could just see what it was going to look like at the end. With that dress, I didn't sketch it at all, and I made it in one day. Even if you can't do that, exactly, take note of what you can easily sense, and remember and practice it as often as you can.

So if you're learning how to make clothes and you have a hunch for how something will turn out, try skipping the sketches. Sure, it might be a disaster, but if you're able to create what you see in your head, that's really honing inspiration. Just beware of the inadvertent copycat phenomenon: There is *so* much fashion out there in the collections that it's hard *not* to see things in other people's work and file them away in your brain. Sometimes I prefer not

FEARLESS TIP:

If you have any inclination toward remembering shapes or pictures, practice doing it! If you can hone that skill, even a little bit, it will serve you well. I actually think my memory is one of the reasons why I did so well on **Project Runway.** ***I can usually remember what a pattern shape looks like. Some people have to take the time to draft a pattern, but I can usually remember the shape of an armhole or a sleeve, so I didn't have to measure it. It was a total time saver not having to measure or calculate.***

to look at clothing, to eliminate that inadvertent knockoff. It's not like you're copying because you want to; you're copying because it's in your head. So if you find looking at other designers' collections to be less inspiring and more headache-inducing, take a break from Fashion Week and browsing style.com; let yourself be inspired by everyday things and not necessarily the new season.

Be Ready to Change It Up

That fabulous, flawless* garment you're working on may end up being something else entirely. Remember the dramatic ruffled neck piece I had in my Fall 2008 show? The one I paired with the huge, wide-brimmed hat that completely hid my model's face? (So fabulous!!) Well, that piece came about in a strange way—it actually started out as a skirt. I'd accidentally sewn it too small originally and I thought, "I've done *all* this work so I can't possibly scrap it; I am going to make this into something!" It occurred to me that some kind of fabulous scarf or neck piece could

FEARLESS TIP:
The work isn't done once you've been inspired. It's also important to allow for changes that come up during the design process.

work, and it looked really cool when I scrunched it all together. I put it up to *my* neck when I was sewing it, and it looked amazing. Who knew? Then, when I was styling the show, I had a small hat on the model who wore the neck piece. But then there was this big huge-brimmed hat that didn't look good with anything else. So after some trial and error, I paired the big hat with the skirt-turned-neck piece, and *bam*! Fierceness.*

Muses

Like many designers, the woman who I design for inspires me. I don't have a specific, well-defined woman in mind the way Proenza Schouler does. So many different types of women can wear my work. One is this chic mature woman who doesn't wear the most outlandish pieces, but she'll buy one piece that's a little out there and mix it into her wardrobe. And I also design for a young woman who's a wannabe avant-garde rock superstar. She's adventurous and she's at the forefront anywhere she goes; she's working really hard to create a life for herself.

FEARLESS TIP:* *Muses are so much fun. It's always inspiring to have a real person to design for and dress.

Paris

My Muses

My fabulous sister, Shannon, was one of my first muses, and I still think about her when I'm designing today. As you know, when Shannon was in high school, she wore stiletto platform shoes to class every single day. She would also wear the craziest clothes you could imagine. Shannon once wore a Snow White costume with lace-up black boots to school! She would pair really odd print dresses with big-brimmed hats, and some days she would dress very '70s. She'd wear really, really wide bell-bottoms and a tiny little top. And with her fierce dancer body and posture, she carried herself so well. With her costume-y clothing choices in high school, I'm sure people made fun of her all the time, but she didn't care. How is *that* for inspiring?!

My model from *Project Runway* and the Fall 2008 show, Lisa Nargi, is another muse. I wouldn't say Lisa is the top model in the world, because there are hundreds of models who are

fabulous. *But* she's so into fashion and understands clothes and design, so to me, she's more of a muse than the best walker ever. She's not just a hanger with a head! Some girls are great walkers, but they're not so into clothing and fashion—they create your illusion that you want to have for your collection, but when you have a muse, they can sometimes carry off a look better because they feel it.

I think that supermodels can be muses, too. They didn't earn the supermodel title by slinking out of fashion shows in baseball hats and Crocs, lady! (Ugh, add Crocs to the *don'ts* list next to flip-flops!) There's the magical power of the supermodel, which has died down a little bit because everybody flocks to celebrities now. But the supermodel is still out there, and she's still a total fashion inspiration. Like Heidi Klum, for example: She's a model, so she's been putting on clothes for years. But she's inspiring because even though she's not on the runway every day, what she wears is her whole lifestyle. Naomi Campbell, too. She's been in every show, she's modeled all kinds of haute couture and worked with every designer there is. But if you see Naomi shopping at Barneys, everyone will have the same question: What is she wearing?! And that's not because she's simply walked

runways in designer clothes—it's because she cares about it. Plus, the way Naomi carries herself would inspire any designer. On and off the runways, she doesn't walk, she glides, almost as though she isn't touching the ground. It's a real sight to see. So these models are all muses in their own way. That's what a supermodel is—not just someone who's standing there putting on clothes with no opinions. All those fabulous girls: Gisele Bundchen and Linda Evangelista and all the old-school models back in the day, like Kimora Lee, (oh, and Tyra Banks was *flawless*!) are inspiring to me to this day.

Models I ***LOVE***

So, as you can probably tell, I absolutely love, love, love models. Way too many to fit in this book, but I have to mention a few more whom I consider to be muses for their sheer fabulousness . . .

Sessilee Lopez

This girl *made* the show for me when I was on *Project Runway*. When I saw her I knew my feathered gown would be perfect on her and no one else could wear it—and I was right. She *wore* that gown. It didn't wear her. I think she's one of the most striking and beautiful models out there, as well as one of the most versatile: One minute she's on the runway in haute couture and the next she's walking in the Victoria's Secret show. I hope she'll be a muse for me in Fashion Weeks to come.

Agyness Deyn

Agyness is supercool and edgy—a very downtown supermodel. She's almost the opposite of a chameleon—she wears what she wears but it's always very Agyness. There's something special about her because her look is so different: very boyish but absolutely beautiful.

Lea Rannells

You might remember Lea from *Project Runway*. She also did my show for Spring 2009. She's one of those models who can be anything: sexy, quirky, funky, cute, whatever you want as a designer. She's not a sassy diva—she's very down-to-earth and flexible. Lea is so good at becoming the vision I have for a show. It's amazing to watch her transform!

Finding a Muse

This concept is sort of like finding inspiration—sometimes it finds you. I'd always loved Victoria Beckham, but it wasn't until she was a surprise guest judge on *Runway* that I really kept her in mind as a muse while I was designing.

But you can look for a muse, too. And often you don't need to go further than your nearest and dearest. Maybe you have a really funny old grandma who wears flowery muumuus every day, but she's also got her pearls and her vintage bag. That's fabulous! If you're a bohemian, girly type of designer, even Grandma can be a muse in a way!

The point is, a muse can be anyone. Your muse doesn't have to be someone completely glamorous—just like you don't need to do crazy, glamorous things to act fierce. You can rock a fierce muse no matter who they are or where they come from.

You can also create your own muse. I think about the Proenza Schouler guys and the girl they design for. Maybe you have an ideal customer in mind when you're sketching. If that's the case, you can always dream up a fabulous diva as your muse! And you can also look at your friends as potential muses—maybe you've got one who wears and looks really good in your clothes. Try thinking about designing for her! And no matter how you go about finding a muse and waiting for inspiration to strike, just keep your eyes open as you go about your day-to-day activities. The more you observe (and relax!) the more inspiration, and even a muse, will find *you*!

16 CONCLUSION: FINDING YOUR OWN INSPIRATION

You don't have to set aside time during your day to go out and find it; just start by learning to notice what's around you.

I like to look at things as random as furniture to get inspired. It gets me thinking about shapes. In that way, furniture design is similar to fashion design. There's something architectural about both fields, and that really gets my creativity going. Either a color on a billboard or a chair in a store window can be inspiration! So relax and open yourself up to being inspired. No matter who you are or what you do, inspirations will only enhance your life—and the fierceness!*

FEARLESS TIP:

Inspiration can come from anywhere at any time and place. It can be anything! Let inspiration find you.

Fearless (Celebrity!) Tip

"One of the reasons Christian was so incredibly successful on _Project Runway_ was that he never struggled with ideas. You'd give him the challenge and _instantly_, his creative process was churning, because he finds inspiration everywhere. He's so full of ideas, if he were to live for a million years he could never execute all of them. The creative process for him is not something he turns on or off. It's constantly happening and, at least I believe is the case for him, inspiration is like a faucet that's always running. He's just constantly absorbing and synthesizing and processing. I don't think he's ever been wanting for inspiration."

—TIM GUNN

A Final Note on Being Fierce

When it comes to success, it seems that all anyone talks about is how to achieve your dreams. But what happens if you're lucky enough to do that? Reaching your goals absolutely makes you feel amazing, but believe it or not, there is a bit of a downside to achieving your dreams and getting exactly what you want out of life. No one ever talks about this phenomenon! But here's what I've learned . . .

As I'm working on this book, I've just received rave reviews for my Spring 2009 collection (my first solo show!) at Fashion Week, I'm hard at work on my Fall 2009 collection, I'm designing costumes for the new Uma Thurman movie, *Eloise in Paris,* I'm dressing celebrities, I've put out a maternity line, and sold out my line on bluefly.com. I'm attending events all over the country, doing red-carpet fashion correspondence at awards shows, and I'm working on some new and fabulous top-secret projects as well. You'd think I'd be on cloud nine, right? Well, I am sometimes, but I do have really, really hard days, too. Some even involve a mini-breakdown and me thinking, "What the hell am I doing? Why am I here?"

Weird, right? I've actually achieved those big dreams I was chasing, and on some days it's left me confused and anxious and totally *not* feeling fierce. Why? Turns out there's something unsettling about meeting your goals at such a young age, and it can actually be really scary. In the past year, not only have all these dreams of mine come true, but dreams that I never thought were possible are coming true, too! So what's the hard part, you ask? *I don't want it to go away.* It can be scary when your dream comes true, because then there's that danger of it ending. When you're just reaching for something you want, the possibilities seem endless. But when you've got it, that's where the stress comes in (and it's really hard to feel fierce if you're stressed!).

Luckily, I got a little reality check from one of my fellow *Runway* cast mates, Victorya Hong. I told her how stressed out I'd been feeling and how this career that I'd always strived for is a lot harder than I thought. She agreed with me. "But," she said, "you're doing exactly what you wanted. What else is there to do?" And she was right. This was the whole point of going on *Project Runway* and trying to become a successful designer. At the end of the day, she reminded me to look at the big picture. Yes, I get stressed about my big projects. I want them to be fabulous* and ferocious so badly that I'm letting the pressure get the best of me. But guess what? I'm not working at a retail job in someone else's store. And I'm not working for another designer toward his or her dream. This is *my* life and *my* dream that I'm living. How great is that?

So now, when I'm not feeling fierce and I'm stressing about what people will think of my next collection, I tell myself, "If everything doesn't go exactly how I want it to, I can always remember what *did* happen to me, and how I achieved exactly what I wanted to do." There are no guarantees in life, but I'm living my dream now, and dreaming up new ones while I'm at it. And that makes me feel fierce again.

THE OFFICIAL CHRISTIAN SIRIANO GLOSSARY

Define? Divine!

Okay, so to be honest, I've never really thought about the difference between a "hot mess" and a "hot tranny mess" before. I just talk! But now that I'm an author, I feel that it's important for all my readers to understand what the hell I'm talking about. So, for your convenience and amusement, here is a handy guide to my favorite words and phrases.

Expired **1.** When something, usually an outfit, piece of clothing, hairstyle, shoe, or accessory is totally over and no longer stylish. The price tag is gone, the date is up, throw your yogurt out because it's expired! Polyester satin—that's totally expired. Stretch silk charmeuse gowns with fishtail train? Expired! They're on every red-carpet event. If I see one more I'm throwing it out the window. **2.** Everything but Christian Siriano designs (kidding, lady).

Fabulous **1.** Anything that makes you excited. (For example, you read in the newspaper that there's a sale at Barneys, and you exclaim, "Oh my God, that's *fabulous*! I'm so excited!") **2.** The utmost level of excitement; the most exciting part of your day. It can be anything from attending a swanky black-tie ball to taking your dog for a walk. If you're excited about it, it is, by definition, fabulous. **3.** WONDERFUL, MARVELOUS (that's one of the real dictionary definitions!). **4.** A word that I really, really like and use all the time! Fabulous!

Ferocia Coutura Ferocia Coutura is that inner diva that everyone has, no matter what size you are or what style you may currently possess. You can name your inner diva Ferocia Coutura, like I did mine, or create your own name for her. My personal Ferocia Coutura was born on *Project Runway*. The other contestants and I were in a boxlike room with no windows, and it just got to a point where my inner diva had to come out. When someone doubts my fierceness, Ferocia Coutura sprays them in the eye with her secret weapon—hair spray. (Aveda Air Control, just like I use!) Your Ferocia Coutura is part of your consciousness—she sits with the devil and angel that many believe to sit on your shoulder, and she may influence your decisions. Plus, she's armed with two cans of hair spray, locked and loaded! *See also:* Ferosh

Ferosh **1.** The state of being when something is totally fabulous but not necessarily fierce. It's often something you do, such as styling your hair a certain way. This can make you extra ferosh. **2.** The doing or making of something to enhance one's fabulousness, not exceeding a fierce point. (For example, "Girl, your hair is looking ferosh today!"). **3.** An abbreviation for "Ferocia Coutura." *See also:* Ferocia Coutura

Fierce **1.** I always say that fierce is not a definable word. It's just a state of being. **2.** The high point of being flawless and fabulous. **3.** Victoria Beckham. *See also:* Fabulous, Flawless

Flawless Often refers to an article of clothing or Christian Louboutin heels. Complete perfection, like a seven-inch stiletto. People can look flawless, as well. Everyone aspires to be flawless, because it's the highest level of perfection.

Gorg **1.** Abbreviation for "gorgeous." When you're being fierce and fabulous, you probably don't have time to say all the words in the English language, like "gorgeous"—that's multiple syllables. So I say "gorg!" Total time saver. And it's cuter, too, right? **2.** A term of endearment; nickname. Alternate: Gorgey Gorg

Hot Mess When someone looks like a hot mess, he or she is kind of hot . . . but not. (For example, "Lady, you are kind of cute and you could be hot, but you're wearing flats and cutoff jeans, so you're a hot mess.") Note: Being a hot mess is better than being a flat-out mess. I mean, at least you *could* be fabulous. It's such a waste! But there is always potential in a hot mess. *See also:* Hot Tranny Mess

Hot Tranny Mess When you're a hot mess you don't deserve to be a hot *tranny* mess, because if you're a hot *tranny* mess, that means you're extrafabulous. Because you're diva'd out. (See my definition for "tranny.") So when you're a hot mess, you're just a mess with potential. But when you're a hot *tranny* mess, you're kinda fabulous! And a mess. All at the same time. *See also:* Hot Mess, Tranny

Lady Pronounced "La-dy!" There is no gender to "lady." No gender affiliation at all. You can be the manliest man in the world, but I call everyone "lady," because everyone has that inner lady who needs to wear full-length gloves and a bird hat. And even the manliest men can be called "lady" because manly men know how to *complain.* If a big, burly man is out to dinner with his girlfriend and their reservation is lost or something, that manly man is probably going to freak out! Whining is often involved as well. So I would be like, "*Lady!* Calm down. It's not like you lost your purse or something!" Use of "lady" can be quite useful in taking the men in your life down a peg. It's a way of saying, "Calm down, you're not on your high horse right now, we're out to dinner, it's not the end of the world."

On Point Use as punctuation (for example, "And then I went to Bora Bora in my new bikini! On point."), or to indicate that someone is really on her game, ready to rock, and fabulous. She's wearing her heels and mini, and her hair and makeup's done. She is *on point.* (For example, "Victoria Beckham is so inspiring because she wore this ruffled minidress the other day and she was *on point,* sister!") *See also:* Fabulous

Tickity Tack A cooler way to communicate the idea that something is tacky. Tacky isn't a cool word anymore. Tickity tack is being tacky, trashy, WT (white trash, lady). (For example, "Girl, that expired pink satin prom dress that you bought for $29.99 is total tickity tack!") Nobody uses "tacky" anymore. Don't say that. Use "tickity tack" because it's more fun. Alternate: Tickity-Tick-Tack. *See also:* Expired, Tick-Tack-Toe

Tick-Tack-Toe **1.** When all of your tackiness has come together and created a perfect score. You won, you have three Xs in a row. (For example, "Tick-Tack-Toe, girl. You are tickity because your hair's in a bun with a scrunchie. You are tack, because you're wearing flip-flops with jewels on them. And you're toe because you're wearing a polyester gown. Tick-tack-toe, girl, you just won. But actually, you lost.") **2.** There's a second definition for this phrase because "tick-tack-toe" can also be used when something's really funny and cheesy—in a good way. Cheesy movies that you love, like *Romy and Michele's High School Reunion* and *Glitter* (Hey, it's good!), can be tick-tack-toe. Alternate: Tickity-tack-toe *See also:* Tickity Tack

Tranny To avoid any confusion, "tranny" is *not* a derogatory term about transsexuals, transvestites, or transgender people. Some of my best friends are trannies, and I think they're fabulous! Here's my take on the word: **1.** Some trannies are really fierce and walk around with stiletto heels on all day long and with a face for days. That's a special kind of being fierce and fabulous. It's tranny! (For example, you're sitting in your office, wearing Christian Louboutin heels, holding your big, fabulous bag, and you just put on a bunch of new M•A•C makeup, and you say, "I'm total tranny greeting someone, similar to "babe," "honey," "dude," or "bro." (For example, from the fabulous *Saturday Night Live* sketch about me: "Hey, tranny! It's tranny.") **3.** Term of endearment. **4.** An adjective that applies to something that looks totally decked out. (For example, from *Project Runway*: "[That fabric] looks like tranny ice cream!") **5.** Can also be used to describe something that conjures up the image of a drag queen at a drag show who didn't bother to shave her legs or wears bad pantyhose or a bad outfit. Trannies are usually fabulous but can, in some cases, take a turn for the worse. *See also:* Hot Tranny Mess

Transylvania The place where all true trannies come from. Transylvania is where you find your inner diva. And when you come out from Transylvania and cross the border, when you get to the other side you get an eyebrow pencil to mark the occasion! (For example, from *Saturday Night Live*: "You're a tickity-tack tranny, hot mess, outta control supertranny from Transylvania who is not apologizing for it!" Ha!) *See also:* Tranny, Hot Mess, Hot Tranny Mess

Trust Often pronounced with two syllables: "Tuh-rust!" It means "trust me" but it's a quick abbreviation. It can, and should, be used as punctuation. (For example, "Oh my God, this spread in *Elle* magazine is flawless! I am *so* ferosh in it. Trust.") Plus, if you're so busy being fierce and fabulous, you don't have time to say "trust me." So you should just say "trust." Besides, used car salesmen and other yucky people say "trust me." It's supershady. Don't be shady, lady, be fabulous instead!

Work Short for "Work it out, tranny," or "You better work!" The word means "do it." And do it fabulous. Get it done. Feel free to use "work" as punctuation. (For example, "I think you should wear your Christian Siriano dress to the party, girl. Work!")

DISCLAIMER: There are no absolute guarantees as to the meanings of all these words and phrases. I tend to change some of their meanings from time to time! So consider these definitions to be fluid, and take it all with a big, fabulous grain of salt, divas, and feel free to incorporate these words into your own vocabulary. Wouldn't that be fabulous? Work!

ACKNOWLEDGMENTS

Oh my God, I have so many people to thank. I wouldn't be where I am today without a small army! So here goes, a big, fabulous THANK YOU to . . .

Beth de Guzman, Sara Weiss, Sarah Sper, and all the amazing divas at Grand Central Publishing. It's always been a dream of mine to have a book—thanks for letting me do it in my own style.

Mariah Chase and Marc Beckman from Designers Management Agency. Thank you for being so supportive and knowing that I am the most crazy, detail-oriented psycho control freak ever . . . and putting up with me anyway. Love you forever!

Matt Horowitz at William Morris, for making sure that everything in my life is taken care of. You take all my worries away!

The fabulous Rennie Dyball for calling me every day in order to write the most fabulous book ever written in English literature—about the most amazing subject! (And for being a superdiva in heels!)

Lauren Zalaznick and Andy Cohen at Bravo. I literally would not be here without you. And to Victoria Brody and Emily Roberts for working so hard, and to all the fabulous little people at Bravo!

The Weinsteins, for everything. You are my divas.

The coolest guys in the world, Rich Bye and Michael Rucker at Magical Elves, for making the most amazing television and creating the best "fierce" montage ever in life!

Jane Cha, Desiree Gruber, and everyone else from Full Picture, for being the most fabulous, supportive divas I know.

To everyone at *Project Runway*, including:

Tim Gunn. You are the best mentor that anybody could ever have. Even if I didn't always agree with your advice, I always admired your knowledge. Thank you for being one of the most understanding people in the world. Hope you'll be part of every show and collection I ever have. Love you forever!

Miss Fabulous herself, Heidi Klum. You calling me "über fierce" was like a dream come true. You are one of the last true supermodels!

Nina Garcia. Thank you for being so supportive after my win. You've given me such guidance and inspiration. Thanks for being one of the most stylish, talented women in the industry!

Michael Kors, for being yourself and always giving the best advice!

All the season four *Project Runway* contestants for pushing me to be the best designer I can be. I love you all!

Victoria Beckham, for basically launching my career by loving my collection! You've always been my number one, most stylish icon, and working with you was like a dream. Thank you so much for your support.

Amy Poehler, for also changing my entire career! Your Christian Siriano spoof on *Saturday Night Live* was a real honor, and the most fun thing that has ever happened to me.

Whoopi Goldberg, for being the most down-to-earth, real person I've ever met. And for showing your sexy legs at the Tony Awards!

Becki Newton. Seeing how you transform into character is such an inspiration to me. Thanks for being fierce!

Vanessa Williams, for being a true, fierce diva. Thanks for sending me the most beautiful flowers! I'll always remember getting to work with you.

Rebecca Romijn, for always being fabulous. And for always being a hot tranny mess!

Kimberley Locke, for believing in me and being such an honest and true person.

Niki Taylor, for being a superfierce diva. After all you've been through in your life, you always come back on top and work the runway—thanks for the inspiration.

Rachel Zoe. I totally look up to and admire you. Thanks for all your style inspiration and being a diva fashionista!

Rachel Bilson, for being the most savvy and cute fashion icon, and for managing to stay fabulous!

Lisa Nargi, for supporting me and being a total fashion muse—not just a hanger with a head! No one could have pulled off my clothes like you. You are fabulous!

My best friend, Sam Bennett, for always being a shoulder to cry on and someone who was there for me in a crunch when I needed to make Whoopi's outfit in two days!

Andrew Roffe, for being my ultimate "handmaiden" and for helping me with every single thing that I do. I know you'll always be there to support me in every which way. And thank you for producing the most fabulous person in the world: your daughter, Sarah Roffe!

Sarah Roffe, for being one of my best true friends in the world and a Park Avenue princess to the end. You and our BFF Jaime Held are the ultimate inspiration for fabulousness.

All the fabulous divas at Bubbles hair salon, for raising me from a little boy into a true fashion diva. Thank you to all of the fabulous stylists who have ever cut my hair, Ann Katner, Jennifer

Mapp, Heather Cravens, Jamie Sugg, and Darlene Smith, because I know that I am a piggy bitch!

(Phew, this is like my Oscar acceptance speech! Or like I just won a Tony*! Fabulous!)*

My teachers in high school. Thank you Steven, Kim, Kirsten, Diane, Nanny, and Leslie, for always supporting such an eccentric young student. You let me be myself and didn't ever question my goals or dreams!

My teachers in college. Thanks to Christiane, who taught me almost everything I know about clothing construction. I love you for that! To Darren, Jill, and Chris, for always believing in my design style and pushing my ideas. To Prudence, for being super chic and fabulous, and teaching me that fashion is hard work.

The Ferguson family. Thank you Liz, Sarah, Peggy, and Bob. You are my family away from home. Thanks for taking me in and letting me be creative, and always loving me no matter how crazy my life decisions were—even when I said, "Let's play dress-up!"

Chuck Phipps, for being my friend and my form of entertainment growing up!

Ericka Sabath, for wearing six-inch stilettos to work every day and never complaining. You were evil fierceness at the salon!

Suzy and Angie, for all the support and love, and for giving me a job when I was *so* poor!

Leanne, for being my model for *Project Runway* and waiting in the cold in heels for hours. And thanks to Nicole, for waiting at Starbucks for hours while Leanne and I were in the audition!

Micole, for supporting my dream, even when you don't get paid.

Candy St. John. Thank you for letting me be your second son when my mother drove me crazy!

Sue, for the walks on the beach in not-so-cute shoes.

My sister, Shannon, for being the ultimate fashion diva muse and for wearing your stilettos and platform heels every single day of high school and college. (You're the reason I'm obsessed!)

My mommy, for always letting me be who I am, no matter what. Thank you for never saying no, never holding me back, and just letting me be me.

My dad, for always being a loving support no matter what. Thank you for thinking *everything* I ever did was totally fabulous.

Brad Walsh. You are the one person who never changed when my whole life changed. Thank you for supporting me from day one of this craziness!

My grandparents, for loving and supporting me through everything, crazy times and all. To my uncle David for being a support in every which way, for letting me follow my dreams, and always being there for me when I needed to talk. And to Grandma Margie in Kansas, where my true *Wizard of Oz* love for life began!

My fans, for supporting a young designer and creating a superhuman out of me! I love you, and you will always be fierce to me!

PHOTO CREDITS

Unless otherwise indicated below, photos throughout the book, including the front and back endpapers, are Brad Walsh originals.

Page i, second row, middle image: Thomas Concordia/Wire Images/ Getty Images. Third row, second image from left; Andrew H. Walker/ Getty Images Entertainment/Getty Images. Third row, fourth image from left; Damien Meyer/AFP/Getty Images. Pages ii–iii, second row, third image from left; Dan Lecca. Second row, fifth image from left; Dan Lecca. Page ix: Dan Lecca. Page xii: Dan Lecca. 11: From Christian Siriano's personal collection. 21: Dan Lecca. 37: Jeff Kravits/Film Magic/Getty Images. 55: Dan Lecca. 57: Chris Moore/Catwalking/ Getty Images. 81: Jason Merritt/Film Magic/Getty Images. 91: Thomas Concordia/Wire Images/Getty Images. 105: Dan Lecca. 106–107: Lisa Graham. 111 (inset): Courtesy of Bubbles Salon. 112: Christian Siriano's personal collection. 113: Courtesy of Bubbles Salon. 131: Thomas Concordia/Catwalk/Getty Images. 133: © American Broadcasting Companies, Inc. 139: Courtesy of Bubbles Salon. 146: Mathew Young. 149: Dan Lecca. 155: Simon James/Wire Images/Getty Images. 162: Dan Lecca. 179: Ingram Publishing/Puresock/Getty Images. 181: Jeffrey Mayer/Wire Image/Getty Images. 191: M. Freeman/PhotoLink/ Photodisc/Getty Images. 193: Matthew Imaging/Wire Image/Getty Images. 195: Andrew H. Walker/Getty Images Entertainment/Getty Images. 203: Dan Lecca. 204: Courtesy of Bubbles Salon. 215, bottom (both), and 216: Photos by Giles Bensimon. Reprinted with permission from *ELLE* magazine.

EXTRA
AT THE
EMMYS